Praise for Adair Lara and *Naked, Drunk, and Writing*

"When I took Adair's classes, which I did over and over again, her enthusiasm and understanding of the process of writing led me to make that quantum leap to being a published author. Now—at last—the depth and breadth of her experience as writer and editor are distilled into this one great book on writing. Every writer should have a copy on their bookshelf."
    —Jacqueline Winspear, author of the Maisie Dobbs series

"This is a really wonderful book. One of the best (and most helpful) books on writing I've read. And unlike most practical guides, it's never pedantic or boring."
    —Janis Cooke Newman, author of *Mary*

"*Naked, Drunk, and Writing* is smart, funny, and very useful. A lot of the ideas in the book caused me to slap my metaphorical forehead and say, 'Why didn't I think of that?' Alas, though, there are no naked writers in this book, except that we're all naked under our clothes."
    —Jon Carroll, columnist, *San Francisco Chronicle*

"The insights are terrific and so is the voice: funny and self-deprecating, ballsy and enthusiastic."
    —Tracy Johnston, author of *Shooting the* ~~~

"*Naked, Drunk, and Writing* is jus~ ~~~
generous. It's truly juicy with co~~~
methodical. The examples are exu~~~
    —Joan Frank, author of *In Env~~~ ~~~ The Great Far Away*

"I started reading *Naked, Drunk, and Writing* and kept reading and kept reading. It's full of good advice and techniques; I intend to steal from it outrageously."
      —Don Fry, national writing coach

"[Adair's] books are wise, witty, and wonderful. This is an author who understands humanity. Reading Adair Lara is a pleasure, but not a guilty one, because we come away knowing not only about Adair, her friends, and family, but especially more about ourselves. This woman makes us think!"
      —Elaine Petrocelli, owner of Book Passage

"Half the people I know seem to have taken classes and workshops with San Francisco's legendary writer and teacher Adair Lara. She is very savvy and smart and hugely entertaining. I admire her greatly."
      —Anne Lamott, author of *Bird by Bird*

NAKED, DRUNK, AND WRITING

Other Books by Adair Lara

The Granny Diaries (Chronicle Books, 2008)

The Bigger the Sign, the Worse the Garage Sale (Chronicle Books, 2007)

You Know You're A Writer When . . . (Chronicle Books, 2007)

Oopsie! Ouchie! (Chronicle Books, 2004)

Normal Is Just a Setting on the Dryer (Chronicle Books, 2003)

Hanging Out the Wash (Red Wheel Weiser Books, 2002)

Hold Me Close, Let Me Go (Broadway Books, 2001)

The Best of Adair Lara (Scottwall Associates, 1999)

At Adair's House (Chronicle Books, 1995)

Welcome to Earth, Mom (Chronicle Books, 1992)

ADAIR LARA

NAKED, DRUNK, AND WRITING

Shed Your Inhibitions and Craft a Compelling Memoir or Personal Essay

TEN SPEED PRESS
Berkeley

For my students, who have taught me

so much about writing and about life.

Thank you for trusting me, and one another,

with your stories.

Copyright © 2010, 2009 by Adair Lara

All rights reserved.
Published in the United States by
Ten Speed Press, an imprint of the
Crown Publishing Group, a division of
Random House, Inc., New York.
www.crownpublishing.com
www.tenspeed.com

Ten Speed Press and the Ten Speed Press
colophon are registered trademarks of
Random House, Inc.

Originally published in the United States
by Scottwall Associates, San Francisco,
in 2009.

Library of Congress
Cataloging-in-Publication Data

Lara, Adair.
  Naked, drunk, and writing: shed your
inhibitions and craft a compelling memoir
or personal essay / Adair Lara. — Rev. ed.
    p. cm.
  Originally published: San Francisco :
Scottwall Associates, 2009, under title
Naked, drunk, and writing: writing essays
and memoirs for love and for money.
  Includes bibliographical references and
index.
  Summary: "A guide that shows writers
how to create a compelling memoir
or personal essay, with advice on structure,
technique, revision, publication, and
conquering writer's block"—Provided by
publisher.
  1. Autobiography—Authorship.
  2. Essay—Authorship. 3. Biography as a
literary form. I. Title.
  PE1479.A88.L37 2010
  808'.06692—dc22

                                    2010022650

ISBN 978-1-58008-480-2

Printed in the United States of America

Cover design by Katy Brown
Text design by Toni Tajima
Cover photograph copyright © by
Chas Ray Krider / fStop / Getty Images

10 9 8 7 6 5 4 3 2

Revised Edition

CONTENTS

PART I
WRITING DOWN YOUR STORIES

one

THAT WHICH IS MOST PERSONAL IS MOST COMMON

I should not talk so much about myself
if there were anybody else whom I knew as well.

—HENRY DAVID THOREAU, *WALDEN*

BY THE TIME I passed thirty, I got it: I was not going to be a writer. Sure, I had impressed my sixth-grade teacher with my heroic dog stories, but now I couldn't finish anything without balling it up in discouragement. So I did the next best thing and went after a job in a related field. I interviewed to be a copy editor at *San Francisco Focus*, the local city magazine, swearing to the managing editor that I wasn't a writer, that my happiness lay in making sure that the absence of "h" in Natan Katzman's name in the masthead was not an error.

I got the job. Pleased to my rope sandals to be hired at a real magazine, I proofread, fact-checked, and coded manuscripts for the typesetter. I sweated over the captions that came my way as if they were *War and Peace*, and wrote headlines such as "Swell Wines at Swill Prices" (which they rejected, the cowards). I called up writers to say things like, "Listen to this paragraph and see if you can live without the last two sentences." I told myself it was terrific to be an editor, enjoying all those lunches out and wearing all those black outfits. All the time, though, I yearned to be one of the writers who came and went at odd hours, looking as if they had tramp streamers moored outside, or who had just left wintry palaces, and gave us their copy to edit.

My friend Cynthia, the production editor, wanted to be a writer as much as I did. She was as thin as a butter knife and wore her sweaters down to her knees. Sometimes after work, hungover from a long day of polishing other people's sentences, we'd go to the bar to drink expensive red wine that we couldn't afford and sorrow over our lot, destined as we were to slave over the scribblings of hacks while we ourselves went unpublished and unrecognized.

It was at one of these visits to the bar that we hatched an idea: We would start a writing club. The plan was simple: We'd write 500 words every weekday and give them to the other person. We'd mark the parts we liked in the other's pieces with a yellow highlighter before returning them. I had gotten the idea from a teacher at windy San Francisco State years before. On everybody's homework, he marked passages that caught his eye with a yellow highlighter. When the papers were turned back, everybody in the class had something—at least a paragraph or two—to feel proud of.

Cynthia was game. We scribbled a list of topics on a bar napkin: parking, rain, first dates, and father. And we were off. We handed our 500 worders to each other over the cubicle walls at work, fished them out of our purses at staff meetings, and brought them with us in our gym bags to our Friday night Rhythm & Motion class in the Haight.

It didn't matter what the 500 words were—we could copy them from the yellow pages or the back of the Cheerios box if we wanted to. I'd rarely shown my work to people before, outside of school, because you only showed people stuff you thought was good. Now I gave Cynthia any old dashed-off thing—not because it was good, but because it was *due*. When Cynthia gave my pages back, I'd read the sentences she'd highlighted, swooning with admiration for my own brilliance. Even if there was only one sentence bathed in yellow, suddenly my head was too big to fit through doorways. *I wrote that!* I was willing to rewrite the whole piece now that I knew I had it in me to come up with that sentence.

Her jotted "I love this!" gave me back the confidence I'd had as child, when I'd scrawled those dog stories with a thick carpenter's pencil, tearing the paper in my haste. I realized that I'd been missing the necessary other half of the writing process: the pleased reader. It was as if I'd been trying to tell myself I was a good cook, but without ever asking anyone to dinner.

Cynthia and I began sending the pieces we wrote to the *San Francisco Chronicle* Sunday Punch, which then published first-person pieces by freelancers, and they began to be accepted. I was so excited at having a byline in the section that got more jam stains and crumbs on it than anything else in the Bay Area that I'd talk the proprietor at the corner store into selling me the Sunday paper early. "The sports page not here yet!" he'd object, and I'd have to practically jerk the thing out of his hands. I'd stand there on the sidewalk, forcing people to go around me, while I read my own piece—or rather my own name— over and over, with a joy that seemed to start in my toes.

It turned out that somebody on the *Chronicle* staff was reading those pieces, too. At a party, I met features editor Rosalie Wright. She greeted me warmly and said she'd been following my humor pieces in the Sunday section. "She's better than Anna Quindlen," she said to her companion, who rattled the ice cubes in his glass in bored answer.

Three months later, dopily dressed in a velvet-jogging outfit (it was 1989), I drove my beat-up VW convertible to the historic old *Chronicle* building at Mission and Fifth streets and parked in the garage nearby. Rosalie met me in the lobby, tiny and neat in a pale blue suit, and we took the elevator to the third-floor office of Bill German, the editor-in-chief who had to approve my hire. Nervously, I followed Rosalie into a large office paneled in dark wood where a gray-haired man in shirtsleeves sat reading at a desk in the middle of the room. German had a large square face. He told me he was hoping I didn't plan to get rich doing this and asked how many columns a week I thought I could write.

Rosalie and I hadn't talked about that. I said, "Three?"

Thank god we settled at two.

I had a question. German was already turning back to the papers on his desk. He was hard of hearing, so I had to shout.

"What should I write about?" I yelled.

He waved impatiently. "Write about your life."

I drove home in a daze to my latest crappy apartment, this one on Waller Street. My two kids were at their dad's next door. I was so happy that I kept walking from room to room, from the tiny kitchen overlooking a dime-sized backyard to ten-year-old Morgan's room down the hall, with its sea of garments covering the floor (she liked to be able to see all her clothes at once). I had to call Neil, the boyfriend I had just broken up with, so I could tell him. We made up and got back together—thus providing me with several months' worth of material before we came to our senses and split up again.

For the next twelve years, my column appeared on the back page every Tuesday and Thursday. What a crucible for a writer! I learned so much. It was a wonderful, terrifying gig. When I got that column, I had nowhere to run, nowhere to hide. It was a personal column, which meant that I wrote about whatever touched my own life: If I wanted to talk about teenage smoking, I had to mention the twin tendrils of smoke in the sky above my own two kids. When my dad, drugged by a prescribed tranquilizer, landed in a nursing home and almost died, I wrote about medications and the elderly. When I made pancakes for my boyfriend, and he said, "Kind of thick, aren't they?" I wrote a column on nagging. When I married again, I wrote about that.

My columns weren't what many of the *Chronicle* faithful were used to. Not all of them understood why I was telling the world how it felt when the smell of yet another smoked clutch filled my Toyota, about the new iciness between my mother and me, about having an ex-husband living upstairs. One wrote to say, "I wish you would explain the purpose of your column." Later he helpfully clipped my columns and mailed them to me with the "I's" and "me's" circled in red, to let me know I was talking about myself again.

I didn't blame him. It *was* odd to be reciting the events of my own life in a paper. When I felt embarrassed to be talking about myself,

I clung to Jung's idea that, ironically, the more intensely individual a person's thoughts are, the more uniquely applicable to him or her, the more they will have meaning for other people. "That which is most personal is most common," he said. Meaning, that if there's any justification for telling personal stories, it's that every person, every selfish little clod of ailments and grievances—including you, including me—contains within himself the entire human condition.

What goes on between a writer of personal true-life stories and the person who reads them is like a friendship—and real friendship is exchanging secrets, taking hostages, rolling over like a dog and exposing your soft throat. You tell your friend things you wouldn't tell anyone, things that you wouldn't want the people at the next table to overhear, and you feel the friendship growing, like a bank account, with each story you tell and each story you hear. The reader hears how you flew across the country to see your 87-year-old father, how the two of you sat up late drinking Scotch, and how you suddenly blurted out, "I think I came here to tell you I love you," and then burst into tears. How it was the last time you saw him alive, and how glad you were that you made the trip.

There's also naturalness, an honesty, to personal writing that I like. It stops argument. When I talked about how I felt when I had an abortion at seventeen, no one could argue with me. No one could deny the experience I'd had or that I felt about it the way I did.

So it was a lucky dovetailing of what I liked to write about—the ordinary, the personal—and an era just about to be born, one that blazed with interest in the real stories of other people's lives. Personal essays popped up on the end pages of magazines and in newspaper features. What was once the "semiautographical novel" became memoir. Mary Karr's *The Liars' Club* and Frank McCourt's *Angela's Ashes* were about to kick off an avalanche of memoirs.

Beginning with that column in the *Chronicle*, I have made a little cottage industry out of writing about, well, myself, though I could hardly be more ordinary—a middle-aged married woman living in San Francisco. While I was still at the paper, I published a memoir called *Hold Me Close, Let Me Go: A Mother, a Daughter, and an Adolescence*

Survived, about how my Cabbage-Patch-doll-loving daughter, Morgan, morphed into a beer-soaked, class-cutting, thrill-seeking, lying-is-like-breathing teenager from hell. When Morgan, by some miracle, became a lawyer and not a jailbird, and had two little girls, Maggie and Ryan, I wrote a little book about being a grandmother called *The Granny Diaries*. ("What's next?" a friend dryly asked. "*Tales from the Crypt?*")

When I began to teach writing, I also made notes for this book—in which, you notice, I don't trouble to keep myself off the page. It's called *Naked, Drunk, and Writing* because I like that title, and because somebody at a party once remarked to me over sushi that books with "naked" in the title always sell. And also because writing about yourself *is* like stripping down to your Bali bra in a crowd so that others can see the stretch marks on your belly (and be reassured about their own). Writing is a kind of word-drunkenness that makes you want to do that—to take off your clothes and turn your experiences into art, despite who may be watching, despite your embarrassment, despite anything the world and your own self-doubts throw against you.

When you finish this book, you'll know how to write essays and memoirs, how to keep writing when you're discouraged, how to revise your work, and how to get it published. My goal is to inspire you to make room in your life to be the writer you've always wanted to be. As you go forward, I urge you to celebrate intermediate triumphs. Laminate your first published piece into placemats for the family breakfast table. Just finish that piece after twenty drafts? Look around to make sure you're alone, bring your elbow sharply back to your side and make a fist—Yes!—and then walk sedately out of the room. When you nail a difficult paragraph, lock yourself in the conference room, put your feet up, and reward yourself by reading poetry for an hour (one of my favorites is Archibald MacLeish's "Not Marble Nor the Gilded Monuments").

Test your progress not against the outside validation of being published but against what you have learned about good writing. Am I using more images? Am I more focused? Are my themes deeper, better developed? Am I forming writerly habits? And most important—am I still having fun?

HOT HEART, COLD EYE
The Inconvenient Importance of Craft

Easy reading is damn hard writing.

—NATHANIEL HAWTHORNE

I DIDN'T START OUT thinking about writing as a craft that could be learned. I was like a lot of beginners who are, as novelist Marilynne Robinson said, "At first less in love with structure or pattern and more in love with the words in a foolish but sweet way." I was an editor at a couple of magazines that often published the kind of writers I considered "bad": They wrote about health, weekend retreats in May, and vacationing in Hawaii in September, and had no tone, no interesting images or language. The blindness of the editors astonished me. Why did they publish dry little features on pet adoptions instead of the literary essays they received from snotty English majors like me? Could they not tell the difference?

They could, as it happened, but they weren't in the market for painfully wrought masterpieces. The writers they hired did not spend days agonizing over the perfect way to describe the sway of palm fronds in the breeze. These writers knew how to put a piece together, where to start, when to end. They knew how to quote people. They knew how to make the reader want to visit the little inn in Mendocino, how to interest the reader in the story of an unknown jazz player. They had a set of skills that could be learned: they had *craft*.

There's nothing like writing a column twice a week for twelve years to teach you the importance of craft. Like an essay, a column isn't a blog, a blurt, or a blast. It has to have several elements: a story to tell, a way to tell it, and a reason to tell it.

I usually had nine or ten columns marinating all over the apartment, like pans full of chicken waiting for the grill, waiting for one missing element or another. I might have two pages about a bad guy who got caught mid-escape because something was wrong with his car. I'd wait to add the second two pages, which I hoped would contain my point, which I hadn't thought of yet.

I learned that writing is not something you do blissfully, sitting in a garden with birds tweeting overhead. Or rather, you *can* do it that way, but you must work. You start with your hot heart, spilling truth any old way onto the page. And then you bring in your cold eye. The cold eye knows that the piece must begin somewhere, end somewhere, and satisfy the reader with a sense of progress in between. It knows that your first drafts will probably be random, jumbled, and contradictory, but that you eventually need to impose a pattern of cause and effect on them. And it knows that the way to do that is to give the piece structure. I just right-clicked on *structure* in my Word document and pulled up this definition: "a system or organization made up of interrelated parts functioning as a whole."

Think of structure as the skeleton that holds up the work. Imagine your body without its skeleton. You would still have all your lovely parts, but they would be in a heap on the floor. The skeleton tells you where everything fits: where the head goes, where to stick the anklebone (connect it to the leg bone).

Structure is not sexy—there won't be a woman with tear-stained cheeks who grabs your sleeve at a bookstore reading to say how moved she was by your use of setup or that tie-back ending. You won't get letters from readers grateful for all the digressions you took out. But structure will get you into that bookstore. The essays and memoirs you've loved may read like inspired outpourings, but if they've been published, chances are they were painstakingly rewritten in many drafts until, as the above definition says, the many parts functioned together as a whole.

Learning some of the techniques in this book will likely feel discouraging at first. You love—make that *loved*—to write, and now find out it's hard! Improving your writing is like correcting your tennis serve: For a while neither your old serve nor your new one will seem to work. Then the new, better serve becomes part of you. So do your new writing techniques. You produce pieces that are both true and aesthetically satisfying, and this brings you checks and bylines and other forms of appreciation.

In terms of craft, what applies to the personal essay often applies to the memoir, and vice versa—you could call an essay a short memoir, and you could call a memoir a long essay. What I call *theme* in a memoir is *epiphany* in an essay. *Perspective* in an essay is *reflective voice* in a memoir. The essay's *angle* is the memoir's *premise*. Both essay and memoir use scene and dialogue, image, and detail. (I know I haven't used all these terms yet, but believe me, we'll get to them.)

By now you must have realized that *Naked, Drunk, and Writing* is not about peeling off your clothes, grabbing a glass of wine, and joining me in the hot tub for a writing session. It's about shedding your inhibitions and loosening your defenses so that you can stand naked before the truth that lies dormant within you. It's about the intoxication that comes with the terror and beauty of being exposed and vulnerable to something bigger than you ever thought you were. It's about developing the courage, confidence, and skill that will take you through the arc of becoming a successful writer.

So come on in, get yourself some coffee, or tea, or whatever from the kitchen, find a seat, and let's go on.

PART II

THE PERSONAL ESSAY

three

ELEMENTS OF THE SUCCESSFUL ESSAY

In the end, it is my belief that words are the only things
that can construct a world that makes sense.

—KATE ATKINSON, AUTHOR OF *BEHIND THE SCENES AT THE MUSEUM*

Let's start with the short narrative essay. Here your aim is to capture a moment, a mood, or a surprise—not tell us a long complicated story. The word *essay* may remind you of what Mrs. Bernardicou with the baggy arms made you write back in high school, but here I'm talking about something very cool: a short piece that you write in the first person about something that happened to you.

Let's agree we're talking about a piece of about 800 to 1,500 words, to be published in a newspaper, on a website, or in a magazine. I leafed through some magazines to find some examples of these for you. A woman in the *New York Times Magazine* talked about her daughter's anorexia: "I stood in the kitchen looking at the mess and thought of how our lives had shrunk to the confines of these four walls." A woman in *Alternative Medicine* recalled how she began taking naps: "The first time I did it, I wondered what was wrong with me." Pauline Chen wrote a piece for the "Lives" section of the *New York Times* about a night harvesting organs from cadavers that was routine until she found herself working on a woman who looked much like herself.

Keep It Small

Notice that the scope of those stories is restricted: a kitchen, a nap, a routine operation. "Great subjects," said V. S. Naipaul, "are illuminated best by small dramas." You reveal the strains in the marriage when you describe the fight over stacking the dishwasher. The avocado plant that served you as a Christmas tree can show your new life in California. Talk about the day the movers came, and we will get the story of your divorce from what's in the boxes. Short as it may be, an essay can be large in the implications of the truth it tells. You can't tell everything you learned about saying good-bye to people in a four-page piece, but you can tell us about one such good-bye—and express what you learned through that.

You know those nesting boxes they make for kids, where you start with a large box and take out smaller and smaller ones? With an essay, it's the opposite: You start with the smallest box. Begin with the day you asked your father to teach you to paint, and he set you up with a still life of a lemon and a crème de menthe bottle to draw. Work toward the larger: the day you realized you were an artist.

The more specific your topic is, the easier it will be to tell what goes in and what doesn't, and the fewer drafts you'll have to write. On the other hand, the broader the topic is—"the two years I spent taking care of my grandfather" or "my interesting experiences in Saudi Arabia"—the more you're forced to use abstractions and make statements we have to take on faith, and in general blather on, and the more drafts you'll have to write to find the story that you can tell forcefully in a few pages.

It's not just about reducing the frame to a detail, like cropping a picture on Photoshop. It's also focusing on one thing, the one story you are trying to tell. (This may mean being prepared to take perfectly good ideas out of a piece and save them for another day, lest they distract.) And, of course, it's not always simple, that act of focusing. The experience lodged in your memory is fused with other memories. It can take several drafts just to find exactly what it is you want to say, and to decide what events or details will best deliver that meaning. Writing about your life can be like clearing a choked up waterway: you hack and tug until the water trickles through.

Find a significant moment, and then find a way to frame that moment. My student Scottie Ross's piece takes place during a ten-minute period in her psychiatrist's waiting room. It begins with Scottie asking herself why she thinks of her psychiatrist as "this white woman" when the doctor is late:

> Where the hell is this white woman? Whoa, who said
> that? Good grief, I did. Okay, so she's twenty minutes
> late. But still, that's no cause for me to be mind-
> screaming "white woman." I've never called her that,
> never thought of her that way. Let's think about this.

The rest of the essay catalogues Scottie's experiences as a black woman growing up in America, including answering an ad for a baby-sitter, only to be handed a rag and told, "You can start in the dining room."

What Question Drives Your Essay?

As we find in Scottie's piece ("why did I say, 'white woman'?"), a question often lurks at the heart of a personal essay. What don't you understand? What can't you do? These provide great starting points for an essay. In "Death of a Pig," E. B. White asks himself why he felt so bad about killing a pig when he raised it for slaughter. In "Shooting an Elephant," George Orwell puzzles out why, as a British officer at an Indian outpost, he had to kill an elephant even after it had finished its rampage through the village and was harmless.

The question that drives your essay can be small: Why can I not stand to watch my husband lolling in the tub for thirty minutes? Why did it take hundreds of wrong exits off the freeway for me finally to get contacts? Why, when I have been content to follow my husband from job to job and city to city for ten years, am I balking this time? My student Catherine Shepard-Haier published a piece in the *Denver Post* in which her question was: Am I going to take the toiletries? And if I am, *why*?

Write about the Moment Something Changed

Narrative essays show us experiences that have in some way changed you. Let's pause a minute to consider this. Some life events feel huge, but do not necessarily change you. You got fired, you got dumped, you got cancer, or you got treated unfairly. These experiences certainly change your circumstances, and they affect you deeply, and for that reason they feel as if they have meaning. But will they mean as much to the reader? Many upsetting events fall under the heading of, excuse me, Shit Happens. You can lose a lot of time trying to write about them. Did a scheming hospice nurse get herself written into your mother's will and run off with your inheritance? Being the victim of a swindle, or suddenly being poor, is not change, but bad luck. Finding out that people can be rats is not change either.

Practically everybody who gets fired sits down to write a book about it—but what's the story? Getting fired makes you mad, but that's not change. You seethe for a while, make some notes. It feels huge to you, and it is. But being the victim of injustice is not a story. It's the literary equivalent of hit and run. It leaves you still you, just grumpier, more embittered, less fun at parties.

You and your brother hadn't spoken in six months—then he dies. You were molested at fourteen and your mother did nothing to stop it. You become obsessed for years with someone you eventually realize is a louse (we readers realized that on page two). Let me give you an example of a vivid event that nonetheless doesn't show change. My sister Nora told me about taking a cab down a dark back street to a business meeting at a hotel in Taipei when abruptly the driver jumped out and ran off. Nora was left with her suitcase and little blue overnight case in an empty cab. She couldn't even read the street signs, and had no idea where she was. In the end, though, she found her way back to the hotel without much trouble.

"Did that experience change you?" I asked her one day.

"I found out I could take care of myself when I needed to," Nora replied.

"Before that cab ride, did you think you *couldn't* take care of yourself?" I asked.

"Well, no," she said. "I always knew I could."

No change. She was the same confident person after the experience as she was before it. She didn't find out anything new about herself. She remembers that night because she was alone in a strange city, with street signs she couldn't read.

Nora's story is an *anecdote*—a short recounting of an interesting or humorous incident. Anecdotes have a strong role to play, but they don't always add up to an essay, no matter how much time you spend on them. It's funny that your old mother bought a BB rifle to kill her squirrels with, but that's all it is—funny. Same thing with the story of how your addled aunt ordered four turkeys for Thanksgiving, or a telephone operator once coached you through cooking a chicken.

The Greek root of *anecdote* means "unpublished news." That's what they are—brief narratives. An anecdote is just something that happened. Running into Mick Jagger in a sports bar in New York was exciting, but where's the struggle, the change in you? Belinda Hulin, an editor at *Skirt!* who took one of my workshops, put it this way in a piece for the magazine:

> If there's no catharsis, no growth, no change in-
> volved, then you're left with an anecdote—a part of
> some larger whole—rather than a self-contained essay
> or story. Like that of most women, my life has been
> full of hilarious-in-hindsight incidents. But alas, my
> accordion body, my landfill approach to housekeeping,
> my bizarre divorce, my cradle-robbing second marriage,
> my unseemly yearning to become a born-again trust
> fund baby, and the myriad instances in which my

slow-to-rehabilitate smart mouth have gotten me into trouble, are just not going to write. Why? Because I've happily, gloriously learned nothing from these romps.

THE CRAFTY WRITER

You want to write about your anecdotes anyway; they're vivid or shocking or funny. Everybody says, "You should write about that." If you can't tease meaning out of them, group them with other anecdotes to make a story: "My Brushes with Celebrity," "Disasters That Didn't Happen," or "Three Things That Happened That Led Me to AA." Anecdotes that can't stand alone can be part of a larger essay.

Find the points of change (turning points, learning points) in your life, and you will find your material: The time you realized it was a mistake to move to the sticks. The moment you knew you couldn't go through with the adoption. The discovery that you had a twin who died at birth, and how that discovery made you decide to become a pediatrician. A moment of change might be the day you threw your estranged husband's nail gun into the bushes and realized that the worst part of divorce for you was not how badly your spouse behaved, but how badly the process made *you* behave. Or the time your Volkswagen filled with twenty pairs of expensive designer footwear was stolen in Mexico, and to your surprise you were glad, and never again spent money on shoes.

Let's say that you walk over a bridge during a summer thunderstorm. You've always been afraid of lightning. Normally, you would sprint to the nearest building for cover and wait until the worst passed. But one day you do not run. Instead you stand as tall as you can, without fear, and when you reach the other side of the bridge, you've decided to quit your job and go to Africa. Your essay will tell us why you didn't run that day.

Here are some examples of changes that would make good essays. The first one is from a student paper about a dinner date that ended less innocently than it began:

> We walked out of the restaurant and while waiting for the valet to bring my car around, Harold asked me if we could have dinner again. Immediately, I knew it was more than dinner he wanted, and I was shocked as the word "Yes" came out of my lips. At that moment, I changed from a committed, solid wife to someone who was willing to flirt with, well, flirting. I had crossed my own line. I found it exhilarating. My self-image was shattered and a sexy, dangerous woman emerged.

My student Kristin Lund changed the moment she found out she and her husband were expecting twins:

> I discovered I was not in control of the universe. I know it sounds crazy. But I was a control freak. I thought I could see everything on the horizon before it got near me. Twins! I never saw that coming.

Notice that Kristin is not talking about the change in her circumstances—having twins is a change in anybody's circumstances (as anybody who's tried to wedge a double stroller down the aisle in Target knows). She's talking about the change in *her*.

Another example is a friend of mine whose colleagues at *Sunset* magazine threw her a ten-year anniversary party. They paraded around the room carrying a banner composed of every story she'd done for the magazine taped together—thousands of words about redwood decks, blue jays, and table arrangements—my friend thought, *Enough!* and quit the next day. That's a change.

Build the Essay

Let's say that you have settled on a moment of change to write about. How do you shape an essay around that? For all its charm and sometimes apparent aimlessness, an essay has a skeleton, an underlying structure that makes it work. The narrative essay, the subject of this chapter, has the age-old structure of a story. By "story," I don't mean "something that happened." I mean story in the formal sense of the term: somebody (in this case, you) wants what they can't have and tries to get it, and the end resolves the problem.

The narrative essay has these major story elements: *character, problem, struggle, epiphany, resolution.* In between these elements, of course, we get image and detail, tone, fantasy, memory, style and language, and the other elements that draw us into any pleasurable reading experience.

CHARACTER

The character in your essay is you—which is why we want to know and like you. A good story is not simply a series of "and then, and then" events told sequentially. There has to be something that holds the events together as a coherent whole. That something is in fact a *someone*—you. What happens in the story happens to you. In a drama, you would be known as the *protagonist*. In a personal essay, we will call you the *narrator*.

You are the "I" voice of the essay. Cells snapped into something singular when you came along—and that's what you want to get on the page. It's not enough to tell us what happened—let us know *who it happened to*. This is where tone comes in, and images, which we'll talk about in later chapters. For now, realize that "I" is not a lot of information for the reader. You write, "I went for a walk," and the reader doesn't know if you're a man or a woman, fifteen or fifty, Lithuanian or a native of Oregon. Look for ways to give readers clues about who is talking to them. Instead of saying, "I was working all the time," show yourself hunched over a desk eating Peking duck out of a carton or briskly snipping yardage at Calico Corners.

PROBLEM

We talked earlier about the question at the heart of an essay. Another way to look at it is to say that a problem drives every personal essay. If there is no problem, there is no conflict, and thus no tension, and thus no reader. Here are some examples:

```
I wanted my son to get the guitar I wanted, not the one
    he wanted.
I wanted to propose marriage to a canoe instructor I
    met fifteen minutes before.
I wanted a car.
```

The surface concern may mask the true problem, one the narrator is unaware of at the time. In fact every essay about getting a *thing*—from a promotion to regional sales manager to a 61-inch HD TV to the perfect cottage in the Pennsylvania woods—is always about something deeper. It's about wanting respect or wanting to make up for a deprived childhood or wanting to run away.

Thus the problem that the writer begins with can be a seemingly trivial one: I want to get into those leather pants. I got stuck with a cat. I can't find the swimming hole my friend drew me a map of. It can be a mundane concern of yours on the day you had the epiphany that changed your life. For example, the surface problem can be you trying to ditch an irritating boyfriend at a weekend retreat in upstate New York, while the underlying problem (as we find out when you end up kissing another girl in a hot tub) is you realizing you're not attracted to men.

You'll see that the problem, like all the elements of the essay, will be fleshed out in the actual writing, as my student Robert Doane illustrates:

```
I wanted a car. I wanted a car that belonged in the
after-school traffic jam, that row of chopped-down
Chevy coupes and shiny waxed hot rod Model Ts that
clogged Mission Street from Jefferson High all the
```

```
way to the light at the top of the hill. I wanted the
thrill of blasting out "Blueberry Hill" and "Love Me
Tender" on the Motorola. I wanted to have a cheerleader
sticking so tight to my sweaty thigh that she left room
for two or three more to her right.
```

STRUGGLE

If the beginning of your essay describes the problem, then the middle shows you running into obstacles as you try to solve it. Some obstacles will be external: You want a car, but you don't have the money, your husband doesn't want you to have a car, or you can't drive. If you stay with purely external obstacles, though, it won't be as interesting (we can read a how-to article on how to buy a car). The interesting obstacles will be internal: You are afraid of driving because your parents died in an automobile accident. Or you sense that once you get the car, it will help you steer a course out of your marriage. Often the interesting obstacles in an essay are traits or desires you have that clash with other traits and desires: You want to quit your skating lessons, but you want to be a skating champion. You want an uncluttered house, but you don't want to throw out anything.

Often the essay will progress by alternating action and reaction: You try something, you react, and a new obstacle pops up. This pattern—action and reaction resulting in a new obstacle—may be repeated several times, depending on the length of the essay and the complexity of the struggle. (If this process is long and complex, you have a memoir on your hands.)

In "Without Me, I'm Nothing," San Francisco writer Bonnie Wach wrote about her postpartum depression. One action she takes in hopes of making herself feel better is joining a baby support group. This is her reaction, which shows us that she will have to try something else:

```
Even in places where I should have felt some kind of
kinship—new moms' classes, support groups—I was an
outsider. Happy new mothers made my flesh crawl. Trust
```

me when I tell you that nothing can drive a depressed
mom to the bottom of a shame spiral faster than a
circle of blissed-out breast feeders happily comparing
burping techniques, smug and satisfied in the certainty
that they are exactly where they're supposed to be,
doing exactly what they're supposed to be doing. Saying that your infant feels like one of those animal leg
traps, and that you're contemplating chewing off your
own foot to get away from it, isn't exactly the stuff
of baby chitchat.

Bonnie's paragraph also shows how you can develop such an interesting voice that we want to follow you around as you wrestle with your problem in the essay.

Outline the Essay

Before we go on to *epiphany* and *resolution*, let's look at outlining the essay. It's a handy way to get a quick sense of where the piece is going, what to put in, and what to leave out. (Later we'll see that drawing an arc does the same for the full-length memoir.)

A good way to define the problem in an essay as you write is to say, "What did I want?" You can try to outline it like this:

I wanted _____.
I wanted it because _____ (backstory). (This is where
   character comes in.)
To get it, I _____ (action).
However, something got in my way: _____.
I had to try something different, so I _____. (There
   may be several action-reaction sequences depending on
   length.)
All the time I was thinking that _____.
The turning point came when _____.

```
When that happened, I realized _____ (the point of the
   story and what you realize are the same thing).
Resolution: After that I _____ (what you did as a re-
   sult of your realization).
```

My student Rita Hargrave, a psychiatrist by day who now carries dance shoes in the trunk of her car, used this exercise to plan an essay on how she got into salsa dancing:

```
I wanted to go salsa dancing.
I wanted it because I was bored and alone and it seemed
   as good an idea as any.
To get it, I headed for a salsa club recommended by a
   hotel maid.
However, something got in my way: The cab driver did
   not want to drive to a Latino neighborhood, and once
   I got there the bartender at the club was hostile,
   and there were no empty chairs or tables.
I had to try something different, so I asked one of the
   women who was seated with friends if I could use the
   empty chair.
All the time I was thinking that I couldn't dance.
The turning point came when an elderly man embraced
   me, danced with me, and I passionately connected
   with him.
When that happened, I realized what I really wanted
   was an emotional and physical connection with a man
   and to be seen as desirable and seductive, and that I
   could do that as a salsa dancer.
Resolution: After that I found the passion and caring
   that I was searching for in my life. I have been a
   salsa dancer ever since.
```

An outline will sketch the story in the order it happened, but an essay doesn't necessarily have to be written in chronological order. In fact, it's often better to start at a point near the end. A *story* is a series of events recorded in the order they happened, but a *plot* is that same story rearranged for maximum effectiveness.

The end of the essay must in some way resolve the problem brought up in the beginning. Since the problem will likely be internal—the narrator in conflict with herself at least as much as with outside forces—the solution will be internal too. The solution won't be getting the car. It will be deciding to get the car.

You can thus think of the essay in its simplest terms as problem-solution.

> PROBLEM: My husband makes unrealistic marital demands (clean house, sex four times a week, wife stay in shape) one month before the wedding.
> SOLUTION: I realize that his demands are the result of cold feet and marry him anyway.
>
> PROBLEM: I hate the large, ugly dining room furniture my mother insists on hauling from small apartment to small apartment.
> SOLUTION: One day while dusting the French sideboard, I see how it forms a link to our family's story.

Write the Epiphany

The "solution" is more properly called the *epiphany*. This was James Joyce's word for the moment where things change irrevocably in a flood of new understanding. Magazines, more prosaically, call it the *payoff*, or the *take-home point*. In life, it might be called the wake-up call. The epiphany transforms what might have remained a mere anecdote into an essay.

The reader knows you actually lived through the experience you're describing, so he expects you to have reflected on what it meant—that is, the reader expects you to offer perspective. This is where the epiphany comes in. John L'Heureux said, "A story is about a single moment in a character's life when a definitive choice is made, after which nothing is the same." In the last line of Frank O'Connor's *Guests of the Nation* a young soldier who has executed two prisoners says, "And anything that happened to me afterwards, I never felt the same about again."

There are two kinds of epiphanies: *implicit* and *explicit*. An implicit epiphany shows us the change wordlessly. This kind is what you see in fiction, and especially in movies, which can only show, not tell. In the scene at the end of the movie *The Paper Chase*, Timothy Bottoms, after sweating through a year of Harvard law school, to the extent of renting a motel room to cram for finals, doesn't even open his grades when they come, but throws the envelope into the waves. We get it that he no longer cares about his law-school grades.

An explicit epiphany, on the other hand, spells out the realization, as in this paragraph from a *San Francisco Chronicle* piece by Carla Thornton of Livermore, who lost her parents when as an infant she was thrown from the car that killed them both:

> We were together for only a few months, I want to tell them, but I am grateful for what memories I can collect, even if they are secondhand. Looking at you now from across the years may not tell me what kind of family we might have been, but it reminds me to treasure the life I've made, even if I was not the fairy-tale princess I once imagined myself to be.

Let's look at an epiphany April Martin wrote in the *New York Times* in a piece about taking up ice skating in her forties:

> Skating has helped me to reclaim the body with which I spent too many years at war. I stop briefly to reflect on the apparent contradictions: I have deepened and matured as a woman in a sport geared to little girls. And I am now nourished and replenished by a sport whose standards of femininity were once a form of bondage.

> Though I bring to the ice the painful bunions and
> chronically stiff muscles of middle age, I also bring
> one of its benefits: the increased capacity for living
> comfortably with contradictions.

Don't you love that? I've read that a hundred times, and am still moved every time I read it. That last phrase is even alliterative: "the increased capacity for living comfortably with contradictions."

Okay, admittedly, some epiphanies give the whole business a bad name, like the one a guy wrote in a *New York Times* piece about how he had his girlfriend's smelly dog foisted on him, and then how he got to like the dog. He concluded: "Because their emotions are so pure, dogs can often touch the deepest part of us. And in so doing, they might in their own way prepare us to understand ourselves."

That's the kind of epiphany that makes a reader go, "Huh?" You can substitute anything as the subject of that sentence and it will make about as much sense: "Because their emotions are so pure, angry geese can often touch the deepest part of us. And in so doing, they might in their own way prepare us to understand ourselves." (It's a good idea, in fact, to avoid the "we" sort of epiphany altogether, as it tends to make the reader growl, "Speak for yourself, buddy.")

A good epiphany is surprising, not cloying or trite. It doesn't condescend or offer a predigested insight. My friend Wendy Lichtman had an awful thing happen to her: A doctor told her that she was dying of liver cancer. Days later, she learned that she wasn't: The "cancer" the X-ray was seeing were harmless birthmarks on her liver. At the end of the essay she wrote about that scare, she said:

> I know people might expect me to say that the experi-
> ence taught me to better appreciate my life, to savor
> every moment. But it doesn't seem to have worked out
> that way. What I appreciate, in fact, is that *I don't*
> have to feel as if each moment is a treasure. Now when
> I watch my children do their homework, it's not a par-
> ticularly touching experience; it feels, instead, like

```
the normal business of a school night. That normality
is what I'm most grateful for.
```

Let's return to April Martin's piece about ice skating. You say, Fine. I'm so glad this Martin person found meaning in her new hobby. But I don't live in New York, am not middle-aged, was not once a feminist, and don't skate. What does Martin's experience have to do with me?

Well, nothing maybe. But you might recognize a truth in what she says—a truth for yourself, as well as for her. Maybe you, too, have done something that's out of character but surprisingly satisfying, like a student of mine who was violently antigun until she discovered the pleasures of the local shooting range.

By the way, not all pieces need epiphanies. Humor pieces don't. I discovered this when I sent a piece on my son Patrick's birth to *Parenting* magazine. They wanted me to put in the epiphany (you will find magazines are big on this: They want the reader to have that "take-home point"). I tried to put it in—magazines pay well—but it kept sounding stupid. You can't write a piece in which you crack jokes ("I was going to give the doctor one more chance to give me drugs, and then I was going to try to get somebody with real connections, like a screenwriter"), and then stop and say in a completely different tone, "Until you have a second child, you don't know how you can love another the way you do your first."

Opinion pieces don't have epiphanies either: Opinion pieces are not about change. You start out in favor of the return of the martini and end up in favor of it. They're rants or arguments or humor or meditative exercises, or any of the myriad other forms of the essay.

DRAMATIZE THE EPIPHANY

Say you write a piece in which you decide to leave your husband and go into hiding with your child. Saying, "I decided I should take off that night" isn't enough to convey such a crucial turning point. Give us a scene in which you make your decision—when you see the court document awarding the abusive father full custody, or find the bruises on the child's back.

This is how essay writers and memoir writers take the chaos of life and turn it into art—by letting us be there when a change happens. The reader wants to be there when you look at a photo of yourself and realize you look ridiculous in the crazy getups you've been wearing. These moments are important, so load up the detail—where are you when you get those photos back from the drugstore? Do you look down at the yellow bell bottoms you thought made such an ironic statement?

A student of mine wrote a pretty good piece about how time is getting away from her: The microwave clock ticks too fast, her daughter is turning ten, she's turning thirty-five, and her husband has cancer. Then on the last page, she says, "So I've decided to make peace with the passage of time. I'm going to stop letting it beat me up when it's already got my attention."

It's a good epiphany. But what made her go from being someone hyperaware of the manically ticking microwave to someone feeling peaceful, maybe sitting quietly in a rocker on the porch? The piece needs the transforming moment, the event that changed her.

EXPLAIN THE EPIPHANY

My student Evelyn Strauss reminded me that sometimes you have no trouble coming up with the dramatic moment of change, but you don't know why it happened when it did. For example, let's say a woman stands in the hospital room of her dying father listening to the hissing of the machine he's hooked up to, and realizes he always loved her. We see the change in her—she tenderly straightens his covers and erases the Groucho Marx mustache she drew on him (kidding). What made her realize it?

What makes things crack at any particular moment is often hard to understand even after it happens. Evelyn said:

```
I can identify so many moments of epiphany in my life,
but I'm not always sure why they occurred at that spe-
cific time. The flashes of insight and meaning are true
and dramatic, but they tend to rest on months or years
of hacking away at some internal issue. I can identify
```

the exact moment I finished coming out of the closet,
for example—the moment when I released the last ves-
tiges of wanting to be straight. Something really did
break inside of me. I slumped to the floor, I cried, I
shook. But I have no idea why it happened after that
particular trip with the woman I was in love with then.
We had known each other for eleven years.

If you were writing fiction, you could easily come up with what
T. S. Eliot called the *objective correlative*—"a set of objects, a situation, a
chain of events" that produce the emotion the person feels inside. But
in autobiographical writing, you can't make stuff up. One solution
might be to write out the moment at length as a separate exercise, asking yourself questions, until you *do* know why the change happened
when it did. You write until you uncover long-buried memories.

Certainly, you want to offer the readers something. We have
enough inexplicable moments of change in our own lives; we read
because the writer offers clarity on hers. An unexplained epiphany is
all right in a memoir (as it will be one realization among dozens in the
book) but not in a short essay, which one writes, presumably, to offer
understanding. Sometimes the solution is to write about something
else. Younger writers, in particular, can find themselves struggling to
set out in lucid prose an experience they don't yet have perspective on.

THE EPIPHANY CAN BE DARK

The point of the piece does not have to be Pollyannish. An epiphany
can speak of disappointment, or of diminished expectations. It may
show that you can win by losing and lose by winning. An epiphany
can be something bleak, like this one by a student:

I told my mother I loved her and she said, "Well,
I don't feel loved." All of a sudden, I saw that I
couldn't fix that hole. I could send something to
her but if she didn't want to receive it, there was

nothing I could do. This allowed me to get some much-
needed emotional distance. We still talk to each
other at least once a week, but we have a difficult
relationship.

An essay can show that while there may be few permanent solutions, there are moments of clarity, moments that expand your understanding. My friend Joan Frank, author of the story collection *In Envy
Country* and the novels *The Great Far Away* and *Miss Kansas City*, who
began writing essays at the age of forty, has this to say:

> By acknowledging isolation, by acknowledging a fragmen-
> tary life, an incoherent life, you are making contact
> with other people who might feel equal isolation. A
> good essay is a communal act, though I never think of
> that when I'm writing: I'm just trying to get things
> right. To get experience right, whatever the experi-
> ence, is to make a communal gesture. Even if getting
> it right is an expression of disappointment or failed
> expectations.
>
> There are Hallmark cards that talk about apparent
> happinesses and joys. It seems to me to be affirmative
> to take on the darkness. To do so affirms that you can
> talk about almost anything unpopular, unsavory, dark,
> and if you get it right, and have embodied it, you
> have affirmed at least the difficulty of living, and
> that affirmation is solace to me. Always if you get it
> right, it's solace to someone—and its solace resides
> in precisions, not in its pleasing sentiments.

As Joan says, you can offer the reader an ending that affirms the
difficulty of living. A young woman found that several wolves were
attacking her cattle. Her essay told the story of the struggle she faced
as she made the choice of saving the cattle or saving the wolves. She

shot the wolves, but learned that whatever her choice had been, she would not have been comfortable with it. One of life's lessons is that sometimes there is no right choice, and exposing that truth was the point of the essay.

WORK BACKWARD FROM THE EPIPHANY

Once you know your epiphany, you know where to begin the piece. Show us you *before* the epiphany that will change you. Start the piece with you cowering at heights; end with you diving off a rock.

Consider a change that happened to John Fogerty, once chief songwriter for Creedence Clearwater Revival. He was so bitter about having signed away the rights to many of his songs (including "Born on the Bayou," "Who'll Stop the Rain," and "Proud Mary") to Fantasy Records that for years he refused to sing the songs at his appearances. Then one day he visited the Mississippi grave of legendary bluesman Robert Johnson. He stared at the name etched in stone and found himself wondering who owned Johnson's songs now. He thought to himself, *It doesn't matter. Johnson owns those songs*. At that moment, Fogerty realized he, too, was the spiritual owner of his songs.

If Fogerty wrote an essay, that moment in the graveyard would come near the end. The resolution (what the narrator does differently as a result of the epiphany) would be that he starts singing his own songs again. If he ends by playing his songs again, he might begin with the first day he refused to sing any of them at a performance.

In another example, one of my students wrote about being in a meeting in Japan when someone bowed to everyone else and greeted them in Japanese, and said, "Good morning" to him. He realized he would never fit in, and soon afterward left Japan. He could work backward from that to an essay that began with his feeling confident that, with effort, he could make his life in that country.

try this

Choose a story about a personal experience that changed you and write it this way:

1. Show us how you were before the epiphany.
2. Show us the transforming moment.
3. Write an explicit or implicit epiphany.
4. Resolution: Show us what you do differently afterward as a result of the epiphany.

WHERE TO PUT THE EPIPHANY

The whole essay aims itself at the epiphany. It must occur close to the end, because once it happens, you're about done. This is why you often find the epiphany in the next to the last paragraph of a piece.

It's sometimes followed by a more lighthearted final paragraph to bring things back to a less portentous tone. In the last paragraph of the ice-skating piece, for example, Martin dives back into the story and lightens the mood: "My coach bellows across the ice, 'You call that speed?' My dead grandmother can move faster!'"

RESOLUTION

Then there's *resolution*, the element that shows the narrator doing something he would not have done before the epiphany. Noah Lukeman said in *The Plot Thickens*, "A character can feel remorse, and think kind thoughts, and have a powerful self-realization, but at the end of the day, when it comes time to make a judgment on this person, we are left only with the trail of his actions, like dots on a map. Indeed, one would even argue that a realization is not a true realization if it is not followed by action."

In other words, ideally, life-changing realizations change lives. If you realize your boyfriend's a jerk but go on seeing him, you may have had a genuine epiphany, but we'd be more convinced of that if we see you dump him.

FORMULAS?

So that's the narrative essay. I see those raised eyebrows. "How nice! All these formulas! Did I wander into a science lab?" Yes, I realize that Flannery O'Connor said that a good story "resisted paraphrase," meaning that it's not about what happened but about the emotional impact of the piece as a whole. And I know that literary types get all huffy at the idea that the mysterious creative process of writing an essay can be pinned to a board like a butterfly.

My student Katherine Brennan told me, "I can't seem to wrap my head around writing this way. I prefer imagining a story I want to tell, or a scene I want to share, and just writing it. I let the piece itself determine a path, a trajectory." Well, she's right, of course, and it makes me feel bad to suggest all these practical ways of looking at an essay, but, in defense of myself, I argue that personal writing can be overwhelming. It has all the complexity of real life, with its many things happening at once, and every idea leading back to the past. Guidelines, formulas, or outlines help you think about what you're doing, and thus keep you from ending up with a pile of unfinished sketches that you don't know what to do with.

In fact, I am going to go right ahead and give you even more practical tips on essays in the next chapter. We'll look at *angle* and *setup*, techniques that are useful for all essays, and especially for writing humor.

four

WHAT'S YOUR ANGLE?

There may never be anything new to say,
but there is always a new way to say it.

—FLANNERY O'CONNOR

M Y FRIEND Stan Sinberg, then a columnist for the *Marin Independent Journal*, had a big birthday coming up, and he wanted to write about it. Of course Stan could have just blurted out to his readers that he was about to be forty and realized many of his dreams remained unfulfilled. But that would be the direct approach. In life, directness is good. In writing, not so good. It's said that when Henry James received a manuscript he didn't like, he'd return it with the dry comment, "You have chosen a good subject and are treating it in a straightforward manner."

You can't just come out and say what you have to say. That's what people do on airplanes, when a man plops down next to you in the aisle seat of your flight to New York, spills peanuts all over the place (back when the cheapskate airlines at least gave you peanuts), and tells you about what his boss did to him the day before. You know how your eyes glaze over when you hear a story like that? That's because of the way he's telling his story. You need a *good way* to tell your story.

An *angle* is a way to tell a story. It is to the essay what a premise is to a book, or a handle is to advertising, or a high concept is to a movie (dinosaurs brought back to life for a theme park!). It's a gimmick or twist or conceit that grabs the reader's attention long enough for you to say what you want to say. Think of the angle as the Christmas tree.

Once you have that six-foot pine standing up next to the piano, it's pretty easy to see where the decorations go. Without the tree, what have you got? A lot of pretty balls on the floor.

Remember Stan, who had a big birthday coming up? He needed a new way to take stock of his accomplishments when he turned forty. The first few lines establish the angle in Stan's humorous twist on the subject:

```
Listen, I can't spend a lot of time on today's column
because there's a lot I have to do. See, today's the
last day I'm thirty-nine years old, and there're all
these things I always wanted to accomplish before I
turned forty. Like get married. Always wanted to be
married before I turned forty.
```

Stan's angle was that he had to realize all his dreams on that final day of being thirty-nine. No problem with the marriage thing ("I'd had my eye on this woman who came into the health club most mornings at eleven"), but he also had to write a novel ("Fortunately, I have a couple of ideas"), and acquire kids, a house, a horse, and a piano. He was going to have a busy day.

Angles are half the battle, so when you find one it's often almost not an exaggeration to say you are practically done, except for the typing. Stand up, stretch, and go eat the leftover chicken in the fridge. Angles make the rest of the piece easy, because often what follows is the easiest thing in the world to write: a list. You just have to come up with your points and pick an order for them. Notice that Stan's account of all the things he needed to do before turning forty is such a list: he could start with the piano, and then talk about kids, and the piece would still work.

You Have a Subject—But Do You Have an Angle?

When a writer talks about having an idea for a piece, he usually means not that he has found a subject to write about, but that he has found an angle. When I wanted to write about mothers and their middle-aged daughters for *MORE* magazine, I had a *subject*. When I proposed a piece about how daughters start to take it easy on their mothers in middle age, I had an *angle*. Even when an essay is a chronological narrative—here's my story of life as a black woman in America—finding an angle will sharpen it, as Zora Neale Hurston did when she began, "I remember the very day that I became colored." Note the surprise in that statement: People don't become colored; they discover they are. An angle always has an element of surprise—that's the thing that makes it new.

Once I assigned a class to write about the same subject: Barbie dolls. Everybody returned with a different angle. One woman said *she* was a Barbie doll, another talked about how the pressure of keeping Barbie well dressed turned her into a shoplifter, a man said he pretended to hate Barbie—burning her hair off over the gas jets—but was more drawn to her than he let on. A student named Lisa Pongrace found her angle in a remark she happened to make in her first draft:

```
Barbie is regarded to be the standard of feminine
perfection, yet Barbie isn't perfect at all—her arms
don't even bend! She carries out a tray of frosty
beverages, balancing it on the two bamboo poles they've
given her for arms. She can't even curl her fingers.
```

Like the outline of a narrative essay, the angle lets you know what to put in, what to leave out. Now that Lisa knows that her piece will be on Barbie's imperfections, she will focus the next draft on that. If she talks about Barbie's stunning array of careers, for example, she might observe that a flighty resume hardly demonstrates seriousness of purpose.

USING CONFLICT AS ANGLE

Sometimes your angle is bringing conflict into the piece when it needs it. It's not enough to write a piece about how much you like to spend the day in bed. You always have to tell us what's stopping you, or the piece will lack tension and thus have the gripping quality of a Hallmark card.

Often, of course, there is no trouble. The trip was wonderful in every respect, the new boyfriend is heaven sent, you are floating in a sky-blue pool in a Caribbean resort, and your only source of distress is that the tiny umbrella from your drink fell in the water.

One fix is to bring into the piece something or somebody who's preventing you from doing what you want to do. If I want to write about how I nervously arrive hours early for a flight, maybe even get a hotel room at the airport the night before just to make sure, I have a topic, but where's the tension? Who cares when I like to get to the airport? So I bring in someone with the opposite point of view—in this case, my husband, Bill, who prefers that last-minute swan dive into the 747 as it pulls away from the gate.

This is why, incidentally, columnists always cast their partners in the straight man role—to be the "You can't do that" obstacle. You can use the same technique. Bring in a friend, a boss, or a mother (mothers are fabulous for this) to oppose you.

How to Find an Angle

If you're struggling to come up with a compelling angle, here are some techniques and resources to try out. An interesting angle can come from any of the following sources.

THE DAILY PAPER

I collect newspaper clippings that offer promising angles. One is a Miss Manners column with the headline, "A Move to Abolish the High School Prom." For anyone wanting to write the story of her own high school prom, there's an angle right there. Who cares if everybody has a terrible time at the prom? We had to go through it, and the next generation should have to, too.

SOMETHING YOU HEAR YOURSELF SAY ALOUD

I was having Thai food with my friend John when I remarked to him that my husband, Bill, and I kept all our finances separate. "We don't even have a joint banking account." My friend stared as if I had lifted a door in my skin and revealed a howling wilderness where sunshine and a lawn should be. "It doesn't sound romantic, but it is," I rushed to assure him. "We've practically never had an argument about money." When I heard myself saying that, I jotted the idea on my napkin: "Divvying up finances like college roommates can be romantic." That statement contains surprise, so it makes a promising angle.

TALKING THE PIECE THROUGH WITH SOMEONE

"I'm not sure where to start, I seem to have two separate problems, the ending seems weak, what the hell is my epiphany?" and so on. If you don't have a writing partner, follow that other human you live with around the house. "See, I'm trying to write about the plane crash that killed my whole skating team after I missed the flight, and I never understood . . ."

Your housemate can yawn, or keep folding the towels, shaving, or even watching TV—it doesn't matter. It's what you hear yourself saying that does the trick. A few years ago I'd been trying to find a way to write about a dark painting my mother made that showed my six siblings and me at the swimming hole in Samuel P. Taylor Park in Northern California, near where I grew up.

"She painted in all the shadows," I commented to my husband, Bill, as I hung the painting in the hall, "but I remember all the sunlight." *Bingo*. Angle.

WRITING THE LAST PARAGRAPH

You can sometimes coax out an angle by writing a final paragraph, an exercise that's just to help you think. I do this often. In this paragraph you type, "I don't know what I'm trying to say here. What am I saying about my high school reunion? Am I trying to say this? Or that?" Just as when you talk a piece through with someone, if you force yourself to focus on what you're driving at, you find you know—or your typing fingers do.

A REMARK YOU MADE IN AN EARLY DRAFT

A student of mine set down some thoughts about being confined to an apartment in Iran with her sister one long summer when their father was on assignment there. When she wrote, "The closer we were kept together, the more we grew apart," she had her angle.

Similarly, my former writing partner, Ginny McReynolds, a college dean, said in a piece about lesbian potlucks, "It's like so many other things in the lesbian community. For many lesbians, putting a lot of energy into something that is traditionally female seems wrong." Angle! If she used that angle throughout the essay, she'd talk about the potluck, but also add other examples of lesbians balking at makeup or housekeeping or fancy clothes.

A QUOTE

I read a magazine piece in which the writer muses, "I wonder: Do health concerns simply represent a more mature way of hating your body?" That'd be a good angle on the current obsession with health. Or, if you are just moving in with someone, you could play with a remark Robert Kaplan, a psychologist practicing in Oakland, made: the amount of our furniture we bring with us represents how much of our past we're willing to give up on, share, or ignore.

I read somewhere about a mother with a sick baby who says at one point, "It's all very hard, but there's a lot of collateral beauty along the way." That would be a good angle for a piece, as would this line from Salman Rushdie's book, *The Moor's Last Sigh*: "Every child creates the father she needs."

I found an angle for a piece about the messy apartment I shared with my kids when I read the following quote, attributed to Herbert Muschamp, in *HG Magazine*: "We want a place for everything, but not necessarily everything in its place." My piece began, "The upended picnic cooler serving as a fourth chair in my kitchen illuminated what Herbert Muschamp must have meant when he said . . ."

SURPRISING REMARKS YOU HEAR

I once heard a woman say, "I've got four sisters and am always amazed that I'm the only one who remembers all family events exactly as they happened." Another woman I know, referring to a crooked curtain rod in her entryway, commented, "That's the kind of thing it takes a year and fifteen minutes to do." Both of those are good possible angles.

How to Use Setup

Setup can be another effective way to structure a piece and is thus a kind of angle. In setup, you begin the piece with the opposite of where you want to go. (We saw a bit of this in the last chapter, when we talked about constructing an essay by working backward from the epiphany.)

Here's an example of how setup works: One day *San Francisco Chronicle* columnist Jon Carroll was attending a wedding reception and he realized he was boring the bride he was talking to. Naturally, any such bad moment has potential, but a major metropolitan paper doesn't hire people to turn out columns that say, "I had a troubling experience the other day that I'd like to tell you about." In order to write about that moment of humiliation, Jon set it up by starting with the opposite: how nice it is, as a celebrated Bay Area columnist, to be recognized and admired:

```
Nice wedding last weekend. Very fine pizza; always a
plus at a wedding. Lovely couple. Sweet music. Choco-
late wedding cake—why doesn't everyone think of that?
Fans. I don't mean to be immodest, but try to stop me.
I am standing there in my extremely lovely Italian suit
(the kind that causes people to involuntarily finger
the sleeve and say, "I had no idea that you owned a
suit like that, or at all"), eating a nectarine and
gazing benignly into the mystic . . .
```

Then the fall, which appeared near the end of the column:

> I look into Shana Morrison's eyes. [The bride was Shana
> Morrison, the daughter of Van Morrison.] She is looking
> at me with devastating politeness. She is waiting for
> my rap to end. She's done this before—her father has
> a lot of really old fans with obscure enthusiasms. I am
> the old guy at the wedding. My face is close to hers,
> and I'm sure my breath smells of whiskey and cigarettes
> and denture cream, though I've stopped using the first
> two and have not yet started the third.

Just as Jon wrote about humiliation by starting with how famous he is, Betsy Carter, in a piece in *Glamour*, wrote about hanging onto people by first talking about throwing things out. "When in doubt, toss it. That's pretty much how I live my life. I have been known to throw away paychecks and dump IRS forms. The only thing I seem unable to shed is people."

There's no reason for us to know Carter threw out her checks—what do her feckless accounting methods have to do with anything? Those details are there to set up the contrast—throwing out versus keeping—that gives the piece its structure. Without it, you have the direct approach again: a writer tugging on your sleeve and telling you how she likes to hang on to people, from ex-husbands to dentists.

Another example? Virginia Woolf began a piece called "Professions for Women" by talking about how easily she became a writer: "When I came to write," she said, "there were very few material obstacles in my way." Writing was a reputable occupation, she said, the scratching of a pen disturbed no family peace, and paper was cheap. She quickly sold a piece about a Persian cat that brought her into disputes with her neighbors. "What could be easier," she said, "than to write articles and to buy Persian cats with the profits?"

A lot, it turns out. That was the setup. The rest of the piece lists the harsh obstacles that impeded the woman writer in her day. If she had started by saying, "It's hard for a woman to become a writer," and then just listed the reasons, we'd have no surprise.

When you become aware of setup you see it everywhere, especially in the movies. When my husband, Bill, and I watch war movies, and a weary soldier leaning on his rifle starts talking about that little farm he's going to buy when this is over, we look at each other and say in unison, "He's dead."

> SETUP: The dream that shows how much the character has to live for.
> PAYOFF: Oops. Where'd that grenade come from?

Okay, that's a joke, but it's one that leads into the next chapter, on tone and humor.

PART III

TECHNIQUES AND PRACTICES FOR ESSAY AND MEMOIR

five

TONE
How to Assert a Specific Temperament

With first-person narration,
tone is identical to the sound of the narrator's voice.

—MADISON SMARTT BELL

I T IS not enough for writing to be clear, well-organized, and thoughtful. Say you pick up an article that says, "Ten Easy Things to Do to Become Rich by Thursday." You *want* to become rich by Thursday. Yet before you finish the article, the magazine slips under the bed. I know that I keep buying self-help books on things from digital photography to good posture but rarely so much as open them. I didn't even use the posture book to balance on my head. Why? Reading them is work. Facts are dry stuff, even if they're facts we need.

On the other hand, we readers devour writing on subjects that don't interest us simply because we like the tone. Many of the readers of Anne Lamott's books on faith are unbelievers, but they charge down to the bookstore every time she has a new book out because they will follow that wry, warm, funny tone anywhere.

More than anything else, it's your tone that determines how the reader responds—whether he laughs, bristles, sits up, yawns, or leaves the room and forgets to come back. As a writer, as much as 75 percent of your energy in revision will be devoted to getting the tone right.

Consider how many ways a person can say, "Where did you get those pants?"

```
Where did you get those pants?
Where did you get those pants?
Where did you get those pants?
```

As you see, the tone you use determines the response you get. Tone in writing is like tone of voice in conversation. It can be amused, pedantic, outraged, sad, sarcastic, bitter, mocking, awestruck, facetious, admiring, or joyful. In fact, tone can be whatever a human being can feel. In a piece on breaking up with his girlfriend, writer Ethan Watters used a tone of regret: "As Sarah collects her books upstairs, I look around the living room. I spot a lamp from our old apartment and run my hand over the arm of a sofa I used to nap on."

Many writers have a habitual tone. Fran Lebowitz has said she writes out of a state of rage. "I think of my writing as an organized and rarefied form of a tantrum," she said. Andy Rooney is always bemused, Camille Paglia adversarial, Gore Vidal wry and worldly, Joan Didion elusive but confiding.

Be careful the tone doesn't slip around on you later—even your sense of humor can take a powder when you write about difficult personal events. You don't want your readers to be smiling at your father's tart replies to his officious nurse, and then shift to "I had been the target of his biting sallies as a child, and I knew how they could hurt."

Writing in a snarky tone at memoir length requires a command of sustained irony that most of us lack. I know: At first I tried to construct my memoir about my teenaged daughter out of good one-liners from the columns I wrote about her. Not one of them made it in: A tone that works in a 700-word column sounds too distant for a memoir, where we generally want our narrator to share honest and intimate feelings. Letting go of that snarky tone is often a challenge for those of us who think we're funny and want to stay funny even while describing difficult events.

> **THE CRAFTY WRITER**
>
> When you write a paragraph that sounds the way you want the whole piece to sound, clip it to your computer. Also, when you are after a certain tone, watch what you read before you sit down to write, as you unconsciously pick up the cadence. It's like being in England and finding yourself saying, "I'll just put this in the car, shall I?"

Are You Funny?

You may not think of yourself as a humorous writer, but that's probably because you haven't tried this form of writing yet. Often my most earnest students, those who have stuck heretofore to Serious Matters, have discovered they can be very funny on the page.

For example, here's a funny sketch in *Eating the Walls*, a memoir about being a single mother by my student Jill Morris. You can tell this won't end well, right?

> In the property boom of the early 2000s refinancing became the buzzword. I realized I could refinance myself and send my troubled kid to a private school.
>
> Steve Garner was the name of the refinance whiz guy in Oakley. (A town that later had the highest foreclosure rate in the Bay Area.) My girlfriend at work said that he was great, like a father. (Neither of us knew anything about finances.) I phoned him up. "Jill, I would love to help you. Let's make an appointment," he boomed down the telephone in a warm, fatherly sales voice. "Jill, you can't go wrong with your property. It just keeps increasing in value. What time can you be in my office?"
>
> "After school, around four," I replied.
>
> "Great. Bring your soul, ha, ha. I mean, mortgage contract, salary, banking details. Sleep well, you are

in great hands." And he hung up the telephone. I spent
the evening nervously gathering papers.

Next day I drove down the dusty two-lane highway 4
to his office. Oakley, a wonderful spread of fruit
orchards until the property boom, was now a mass of
fast-built strip malls and lavish homes. When I say
"fast-built," I am referring to the theatre-wall construction concept. The plywood that you can put your
hand through if you are slightly, not enormously,
angry.

Steve's office was painted a happy white on the
outside with slabs of concrete for steps. I found myself in a room of piped music and plastic plants. A
voice boomed "Hello, Jill! Get her set up, Mary-Lou."
Are people really called Mary-Lou?

Mary-Lou offered me a soda and then said, "Now
stand in front of the plant. We're going to take your
picture."

"Make sure it is a pretty picture, Mary-Lou,"
boomed Paul.

Notice how strong, likable, and wry Jill's voice is here. This is not
an angry diatribe about getting taken in by hustlers, though it easily
could be. It's somebody telling us about a time when she was an idiot.
The details the author includes contribute to the humor: The refer-
ence to plywood hints at the shoddiness of the refinancing operation.
Both her observations (the "happy white" building) and her internal
thoughts ("Are people really called Mary-Lou"?) remind us that she's
no fool, and make her someone we want to follow around, even when
she's just talking about refinancing a townhome.

Next, we'll look at some ways to use humor to good effect in
essays or memoirs.

USE AN INAPPROPRIATE TONE TO CREATE COMIC TENSION

Humor can provide needed distance on searing subjects in both essays and memoirs. In her *The New Yorker* piece "Cancer Becomes Me," where we'd expect a tone of despair, Marjorie Gross surprises us: "So I'm sitting in the doctor's office, he walks in, just tells me straight out, 'I was right—it's ovarian cancer, so I win. Pay up.'"

Notice that this use of an unexpected tone (banter where we expect gravity) becomes an *angle*—the distinguishing feature of the piece. A surprising tone can make a piece work all by itself.

In a piece called "Seeing the Sights in San Francisco," Kay Boyle (later U.S. poet laureate) employs the lighthearted, slightly ditzy tone of Sunday magazine travel writing to describe San Francisco's Golden Gate Cemetery filling up with dead Vietnam veterans: "Last year I frequently suggested to sojourners in these parts that Sunday was the best day of the week to make a tour of the fabulous Golden Gate Cemetery which lies in all its verdant beauty in the rolling countryside." The result, of course, is irony.

You can use an inappropriate tone to keep a sentimental tone out of a sentimental subject, as my student Bernadette Glenn does below:

```
I cried when I handed in my ID card. There went my
whole identity. Home to the greedy sucking jaws of my
kid. I had to face the misery of filling the day with
a boisterous, self-centered little bully who had no
control over his own bowels, never mind his emotions.
I had imagined a small period of rest every day, but he
was outgrowing naps and he drooled on the newspaper and
punched me if it looked like I was not paying attention
to him.
```

Better than her whipping out a billfold of photographs of her little darling, isn't it? A sentimental subject is always a challenge. I wrote a book about grandmothers because I found the ones already out there mawkish and treacly ("Grandmothers are mothers with frosting"). The writers love their grandchildren and say so, which leaves the reader with nothing to do except get an insulin shot. Okay, now what I just said sounds a bit superior, doesn't it? Bad tone . . .

A good inappropriate tone is sympathy where we expect anger. My writing partner Marsh Rose employed this technique when she riffed about a neglectful landlord:

```
Dear Zoë,

I would like to introduce myself to you. In fact, I
often sit in this dim living room—cross-legged on the
floor furnace, praying for warmth—and imagine what
that might be like . . . to introduce myself to you. I
see myself racing into the street, flinging myself at
your noisy green Camaro as you drive by with your gaze
averted, and shouting out the truth about you. "A land-
lady!" I would cry. "A landlady!"
    You know me by sight. I'm the woman in the muddy
boots and rubber gloves who stands in the driveway of
this rented hovel, leaning on a rake and peering up
at the porch roof, gauging with my eye how much far-
ther it's tilted to the left. On some early mornings
when I'm about to leave for work and I'm at the thresh-
old with my purse over my shoulder, I imagine I hear a
whoosh. When I open the door, there on the ground would
be the porch roof in a mound of debris with a still-
settling cloud of dust, mold spores, old sparrow feath-
ers, pine needles, and squirrel droppings.
```

CHOOSE YOUR WORDS CAREFULLY—AND PLAYFULLY

Humor is established by word choice, among other things. When essayist Laura Blumenfeld began a piece by saying, "I was speaking with two female friends recently, and in an instant came face to face with the odious beast that is my soul," the humorous, self-deprecating words "odious beast" established the wry tone. Daniel Ben-Horin struck that same tone in a piece when he began a camping story by saying, "We were three men being Manly Men on a winter weekend in the Sierra two years ago." My student Ellie Spence shows us herself as a pious little brat in this sentence: "I proudly wore a medal of the Holy Virgin pinned to my undershirt. I made sure that the communion wafer melted in my mouth, lest I accidentally cause pain to Our Lord by having His Body come in contact with my teeth."

Notice how Nora Ephron establishes a self-deprecating tone in her novel *Heartburn*, a book that for my money is all tone: "My father's apartment was empty, my father having been carted off to the loony bin only days before by my sister Eleanor, who is known as the Good Daughter in order to differentiate her from me."

BE UNREASONABLE

Writers are not nice. They are maniacs, gripped by unreasoning desires, driven by passions, consumed by jealousy. They are drama queens. (And drama kings.) In the process of becoming civilized, a person learns to conceal strong feelings, fight down irrational responses, and look at all sides of a question. This is socialized behavior. In writing, you want to ramp feelings up. Don't talk about how you're vaguely unhappy in Nevada: Talk about how you're prepared to drink the cleaning fluid under your sink if you have to spend one more day in Winnemucca. If you have the flu, you are not merely feeling unwell: you are near death, and in fact have become anxious that whoever handles your funeral will get everything wrong.

When you're writing humor, you want to sound in some way perverse (unless you're Jonathan Swift writing "A Modest Proposal," in which case you want to sound reasonable to balance the outrageousness of offering to solve the famine by eating Irish babies). You are exasperated, or silly, or unable to keep quiet anymore.

My friend Mark Hetts, a handyman who lives around the corner, made use of an inappropriate tone in a different way when he started an advice newsletter called "Mr. Handyman." In it he offered workaday suggestions on such topics as picture railings, spackling, and best brands of paint, but it wasn't the subject that made Mark a syndicated columnist in thirty papers; it was the tone. Look at his engaging Miss

Manners—like tone of exasperation—which is not at all what we'd expect from a man advising us about mildew:

> The worst thing that can be done (and one of the most
> common) is to get one of those prepared tub and tile
> caulking kits, and smoosh out white caulk all over
> the mildewed places to make everything look clean and
> pretty again. For about three weeks. This is compound-
> ing the original personal slothfulness that allowed the
> mildew to appear in the first place with gross miscon-
> duct, since the caulking compound forms a perfect pro-
> tected environment under which the mildew can flourish
> into a tile-removing, paint-cracking, corner-splitting
> dragon that will eventually cause your house to col-
> lapse around the bathroom.

My favorite use of the unreasonable tone is the rant. Rants can be heard on NPR's *All Things Considered* and *Morning Edition*. Fran Lebowitz (author of "Manners") *owns* this form. Nancy Franklin began a rant in *The New Yorker*'s "Shouts & Murmurs" like this:

> While the rest of you loudly and meaninglessly cele-
> brate the New Year—I'm not judging, I'm just making an
> observation—I prefer to reflect quietly on the
> lessons I've learned or partially absorbed or once
> thought I heard someone talking about as I was going
> down the street trying to get to the hardware store
> before it closed.

That's pretty silly. I love rants. Here's one my student Lisa Pongrace wrote about what she called the "The Holy Grail of Black Shoeness":

> I mean, sure, I could be a sensible, contented cow and
> wear the old strappy, flat black sandals from three
> years ago with the black skirt and the chartreuse top,

but it would be more fashion forward to wear the newer,
higher, chunkier ones. Unless I have to do any walking whatsoever in them, in which case I'd have to glue
them to my feet on account of their idiotic slide-in,
no-strap-around-the-heel design, so that when you walk
you have to squinch up your toes just to keep the shoes
from falling off, and if you squinch for too long you
get cramps in your feet and after all, good heavens, I
am NOT a slave to fashion; I will NOT have crampy feet
just for the sake of a little style.

DENY THE OBVIOUS

In one student piece, the writer says that everybody had warned her
life would change when she had the baby. She declares to the reader
that *tra la*, it hasn't changed, she still does all the things she ever did.
And then we see how far from the truth that is: Her breasts leak in
yoga class, the baby squalls at the Mexican resort, she can't stay out
late dancing because she has to get up to feed the baby at 6 a.m., and
she lugs the baby along skiing and when they're farthest from the
hotel he poops and has to be taken back for changing.

TAKE A STATEMENT LITERALLY

When I asked my nine-year-old where his homework was, he said,
"Somebody stole it. It was right in my pocket." In the piece, I say that
his statement made me shiver. "We live in the Duboce Triangle in San
Francisco. With several schools nearby, it's a favorite turf of the dread
spelling-homework gangs."

FIND UNLIKELY COMPARISONS

A *New York Times* piece compared Staten Island's refusal of New York's
garbage to the breakup of a marriage. I once likened teens to cats:

While children are dogs, loyal and affectionate, teenagers are cats. It's so easy to be the owner of a dog.
You feed it, train it, boss it around and it puts its

head on your knee and gazes at you as if you were a
Rembrandt painting. It follows you around, chews the
dust covers off the Great Literature series if you stay
too long at the party and bounds inside with enthusiasm
when you call it in from the yard. Then, one day around
age thirteen, your adoring little puppy turns into a
big old cat. When you tell it to come inside, it looks
amazed, as if wondering who died and made you emperor.
Instead of dogging your footsteps, it disappears.

Be a Screwup

Most of the time, in personal writing, the tone is going to be fine,
because you are being honest and vulnerable, and because you're the
one doing something wrong or getting something wrong. Personal
writing works best when it has a rueful aspect—illusions shed, mistakes made. As J. P. Donleavy said, "Writing is turning your worst
moments into money."

When you write about how you've messed up, we like you, since
we've messed up, too. A sympathetic, vulnerable, and thus appealing tone is created. (If your life has been one of ping-ponging from
triumph to triumph, keep it to yourself, thanks.) If you tell us you
drank all during your husband's rehab, we're intrigued. If you tell us,
on the other hand, that you made no mistakes during your tenure as
vice president of the country during the Iraq war, we lose interest.
We want the dirt: how you really think and feel, as opposed to what
you're supposed to think and feel. We want to hear about the day your
friend left a telephone message saying she had cancer, and you waited
until the next day to call her back. You may have to mention the "I
Hate Sarah Club" that you and Shirley Matson formed when you were
eight. Or admit that your stepson's mother is hostile to you not only
because she's a jerk, but because you had an affair with her husband
while they were still married.

Phillip Lopate said in his wonderful introduction to *The Art of the Personal Essay*:

> The real possibility of the personal essay, which is to catch oneself in the act of being human . . . means a willingness to surrender for a time our pose of unshakable rectitude, and to admit that we are, despite our best intentions, subject to all manner of doubt and weakness and foolish wanting.

That doubt and weakness and foolish wanting? That's your material. Go ahead, rip the curtains from the windows. As Phillip Lopate also pointed out, "The spectacle of baring the naked soul is meant to awaken the sympathy of the reader, who is apt to forgive the essayist's self-absorption in return for the warmth of his or her candor."

The tone gets tricky when what you're being candid about is those nasty other people. Keep an eye on your tone whenever you're discussing the behavior of anybody but yourself.

FLIP THE SCRIPT

To guard against portraying yourself as the victim of the story or unconsciously seeking sympathy or using your pen as an instrument of revenge, *flip the script*. Make yourself the one who is getting something wrong. Write about the mistakes you made in your friendships rather than how you were treated by your friends. Whether you're describing the sexual abuse you suffered from your older brother or a teacher's cruelty to you, be calm and dispassionate. Assume that everyone was doing his best, according to his nature. Write with forgiveness, understanding, and humor.

WAIT UNTIL YOU CALM DOWN

Often you can't avoid sounding snooty or aggrieved or sarcastic or outraged until time and perspective (and many revisions, and perhaps the tiniest amount of therapy) do their work. It took Frank McCourt decades to detach enough from his anger toward his feckless father to give *Angela's Ashes* its nonjudgmental tone. He said:

```
The voice came one day. It was miraculous. One day I
just wrote the sentence. "I'm in a playground in Kassen
Avenue in Brooklyn. I am three and my brother, Menachie,
is two. We're on a seesaw. Up down, up down." I wrote
in the present tense, and I wrote as a child and felt
very comfortable. And I was on my way after that.
```

You can see this resulting unjudging tone of a child throughout the book. His father comes home drunk on the dole money, blubbering sentimentally about the siblings who have died (through his neglect), and yet the child narrator is not angry:

```
He staggered to me and hugged me and I smelled the drink
I used to smell in America. My face was wet from his
tears and his spit and his snot and I was hungry and I
didn't know what to say when he cried all over my head.
```

A number of people I know couldn't bring themselves to read *Angela's Ashes* because it was too grim: alcoholism, humiliation, poverty, dirt, disease, untimely death. But for me the dry humor throughout the book tempers the meanness and provides hope.

Watch Your Tone

Some topics are going to give a writer built-in problems with tone. For example, a singles columnist of my acquaintance once wrote about the problems of being a size six, and about how, on the whole, she was glad she was straight. She may also have listed the wonderful Valentine's Day presents her equally straight boyfriend has given her over the years.

Such topics are almost impossible to succeed at. When I worked with a rich vintner on the book on her winery, I told her sure, you can go ahead and describe how you chose identical pink nail polish and tiny gold earrings for your Hispanic house staff, and then taught them to put their hair up and take the vacuum cleaner apart efficiently. Later I realized I was wrong: the rich can't write on such topics about the poor without sounding patronizing, period.

SOME TOPICS JUST DON'T WORK

Sometimes the best thing to do is just write about something else. My student Jean, a therapist, wanted to write about taking care of her demented mom, but everything she wrote sounded bitter, one-sided. The rest of us in that class didn't know what a nice woman Jean was until she started writing little columns, and then we wanted to hear everything she wrote, including how she went to a nursing home to recruit voters for Barack Obama and found herself pinning campaign buttons on people in various stages of coma. Her mom was just not a good topic for her.

I ran into another problem with tone when I sent my own mother a draft of a piece about the mobile home park she lived in. I thought the piece was an homage—I loved that park, with its pool and duck pond and a pretty marsh running up one side. But she was livid, and I tore it up. I live in a large Victorian in San Francisco. No way can I write about the trailer park. (I've been forced to confine myself to jokes to my sister who lives in the park, too, saying, "Shall we walk over to the store or take the house?")

TRY CHANGING YOUR ANGLE

If you're very attached to a particular topic and don't want to abandon it quite yet, try changing your angle. Here's a piece I wrote about an expensive (comped) week at a luxury spa. No matter how I wrote it, my superior attitude—*my god, what a self-indulgent way to spend money!*—showed through. The first versions went like this:

> Bill and I feel all tuned up and tingling now, lighter
> and stronger, but still a faint air of decadence hangs
> over the week as I look back on it. $2500 a week for
> this? One hike leader confided to me that for that kind

of money she'd be willing to move in with you, lead
you through exercise, feed you, and read you a bedtime
story.

You can see where this is going: me right, luxury-spa frequenters wrong. Not a great tone for a personal essay in which you're trying to get the reader on your side. I stole a more successful angle from my writing partner Ginny, who said she thought that spas got it all wrong when they offered you a chance to eat less food than usual and then herded you up and down trails. At her dream spa, someone would come to her room and wash her hair for an hour every day. She wanted "sitting on the porch" to be listed on the brochure, as well as "getting all the sleep you want." Also first-run movies, window-shopping, and having chips and salsa available around the clock. Picking up on her idea, I wrote about my own dream spa:

There could still be hikes—I like hikes—but they
would all end at sunny lakes, and the lakes would be
lined with couches, and beside the couches would be
wonderful novels to read, and peanut butter and jelly
sandwiches to eat. The hike leaders would be jolly
overweight types and would make us all feel very fit as
they doubled over to catch their breaths, and merrily
waved us on up the trail.

Adjusting your angle can sometimes breathe new life into your piece and make it work. This is especially true if you're tackling a thorny subject.

STEER CLEAR OF BEING A KNOW-IT-ALL
When you're on the side of truth and justice, or you take an obvious stand (Anna Quindlen comes out against spousal abuse!), your tone can be dull or ponderous. I've learned to be wary whenever I'm expressing an opinion (you know you're doing that when the writing starts to feel like a breakthrough, as if you are bringing the tablets down from the

mountain). In personal writing, you want to *show the experience that led to that opinion*; the actual opinion is unimportant to us.

Self-assured types can be wonderful at opinion, criticism, and op-ed pieces, but they don't make good personal essayists. A writer in this genre should be someone who looks at the world and says, "Tell me that again. I don't believe it, I don't understand." Not someone who has a point of view to get across.

Don't think. Don't philosophize. Feel. (It isn't as if your views won't creep in anyway. As someone said, "You put your opinion into all your art or it ain't art.")

The know-it-all tone is a problem I have with this very book, as you can imagine. How can I shoehorn into it what are—no bones about it—bits of advice, without making you feel lectured to? (In fact, that very use of "you" just now might be dicey.) I noticed that Anne Lamott in *Bird by Bird* took care to say, "I tell my students" to avoid lecturing the reader directly. Did I solve that tone problem in the pages of this book? You're reading it. You be the judge.

Finding Your Voice: Do You Sound Like You?

Your voice is your personality on the page. "Finding your voice" means sounding like yourself on the page. It means discarding the unnatural pitches you experimented with along the way, or that you were taught in school, and letting your natural voice out, that low, thrilling voice you were born with.

It's you sounding so much like you, and so unlike anybody else, that we don't need to see the byline to know you wrote the piece.

try this
Get voice-transcription software and tell your story aloud to capture the directness of your voice. If you have a laptop or cell phone with a microphone, you can dictate as you drive. Write your way to work!

Novelist Lynn Freed described finding her voice in *Reading, Writing, and Leaving Home: Life on the Page*:

> The opening paragraph was the hook of my story. More than this, it was the paragraph in which I had fallen into a voice both new and, at the same time, completely familiar to me. It had taken me back to myself as a child, perhaps, to the sort of provocative behavior practiced at the far end of the dining-room table. Whatever the case, it had brought with it a new and completely familiar way of considering the world—a way of seeing, a way of knowing, that I had never before been able to translate onto the page.

Part of finding your voice is knowing whom you're talking to. Imagine a reader who loves every word you write, is your biggest fan, but is easily bored, who'll gag if you say something sentimental, and won't blanch at a swear word or at what you did behind the hardware store with Bill Hawkins. Jane Jacobs, author of *The Death and Life of Great American Cities*, would try her ideas out on a series of astute imaginary companions. Sometimes she addressed her thoughts to a Celtic novelist called Alfred Duggan who was familiar only with fire and the sword. Everything else had to be explained to him. She'd talk to Thomas Jefferson while she was out running errands, and then switch to Benjamin Franklin, trying to put difficult ideas in simple terms that he would like. "Like Jefferson, he was interested in lofty things, but also in nitty-gritty, down-to-earth details," she told a reporter, "such as why the alley we were walking through wasn't paved, and who would pave it if it were paved. He was interested in everything, so he was a very satisfying companion."

try this

- Pretend to admire something to reveal its flaws. You can admire the wisdom of the city fathers for tearing down a freeway, admire your teenage daughter's scanty outfit (so sensible for a hot climate, if only you lived in one).

- Take any commonly accepted idea and reverse it. Write about the benefits of being mugged, fired, sick, divorced, broke, stood up. About how chain stores create urban charm.

Tone is also created by the images and details you choose. What you notice and bring to the reader's attention is part of the attitude you create. A woman can walk into glaring sunshine or into a bright day—the sunshine is the same, but the mood is not. And with that thought, we'll move right on to image and detail, the elements of writing that are easiest to get good at—and the ones that can turn a story from a stick figure into a rich tapestry.

six

IMAGE
The Luminosity of the Particular

Don't tell me the moon is shining;
show me the glint of light on broken glass.

—ANTON CHEKHOV

THERE YOU are, writing page after page about something that happened to you. You stay up writing until 3 a.m., tumble into bed
next to your twitching mate, and can't fall asleep because you're so
excited about your piece.

Then you show it to somebody, this piece that you're so proud of,
and she says, "Wow. That's so powerful," but it must not be, because
she doesn't even notice that she's reading it with the pages out of
order. What happened? You forgot to put in the images. Could happen to anybody.

Here's what happens when you *do* put in the images. One of my
students wrote a piece in which she described her troubles with a gang
at a Catholic grammar school this way: "The girls in the gang roll their
white socks down around their ankles, instead of folding them over,
like we're supposed to. They never polish their Oxfords either—there
are always gray, metal-looking scuffmarks on the sides. It makes their
feet look like ice-skating blades, sharp and thin."

Does the narrator have a chance against a gang so brazen that they roll their white socks down around their ankles? No. How do we know? Because, as we're shown next, she is so nervous that she over-polishes her own shoes: "I polish mine every morning, leaving crusts of white chalk around the lace holes and the seams."

The writer brings her camera in close—right to the shoes!—and keeps it there. Look what happens when she does: "Their shoes look like ice-skating blades, sharp and thin." "Sharp," "thin," "blades," and "metal." Put those together and what do we have lurking just below the level of consciousness in that sentence? *Knives*!

Did the writer intend all this—the accumulation of menace with each succeeding image? I doubt it. When you trust images to do the work for you, much of what spills onto the page is unconscious. That's why you are so often astonished to see what you wrote (and why you have to write things out so you can discover what surfaces).

Think of how much better the above is than this: "The other girls at school were really mean to me. I was scared of them because they weren't afraid to break the rules and I was." Writing is turning your thoughts, abstractions, generalizations, and opinions back into the experiences you got them from. Not "women my age become invis-ible," but "they handed drinks around and forgot me, again." In all my years of teaching, I don't think I've ever counseled someone to expand their story outward: "This is too full of smoke and fire and sandy floors, blood and moonshine. Can you put in some more abstractions, maybe some generalization, and, if you have time, your opinions?"

We want experience, not information. "Joan was distressed" is information. "Joan looked away" is an image. The reader notices Joan looking away and has the pleasure of concluding for herself that Joan is distressed.

Here's a good habit to get into: Every time you write a sentence, ask yourself, *How can I show this?* You'll be amazed at what comes up. Instead of saying, "My mother was untidy," you'll show us your moth-er's laddered nylons, her shimmering slip with the lace coming off, the lipstick hastily slashed on.

You can start with a colorless factual statement: "The house burned down when I was ten." But don't leave it there. Does the reader really care what happened to you when you were ten? That's just a fact—and a fact about a stranger. Make the reader care. Ask yourself questions about that day (Where was I when the fire broke out? What did I see?) until a scene emerges. A student of mine did just that, giving us a scene with a boy trembling in a cornfield, watching his mother come out of the burning house with a baby in her arms, kicking a rolled-up Persian rug in front of her.

Asking yourself questions is a great technique. If you're writing about running away at age seven, for example, ask yourself: What did I take with me? One student wrote in answer to that: "I walked down the street with my little hobo bundle. Inside the bundle was my stuffed dog, two apricot fruit rollups, a bottle of Orange Crush, and construction paper and crayons. I don't know why I had the paper and crayons, except I remember pulling out the purple crayon, which reminded me of my sister because it was her favorite color."

Ginny McReynolds wanted to say that her mother was older than the other mothers. To show that, she wrote, "By the time all of those other five-year-olds were reaching across sheets of creamy butcher paper for yellow and brown paint to color their mothers' hair, I was the only one mixing black and white to make gray." When we read that, we're not being *told* that the narrator feels set apart from the other kids because she has the wrong sort of mom. We're leaning over a child's shoulder in a classroom and *feeling* it.

Find the images. In one story, the writer describes the nurse's feet when she learns of her stillborn daughter. This tells us, without telling us, that she can't look up. If you're writing a story about a missing child, mention the light switch on the porch taped over so that no one can turn it off, ever. This will tell us more than anything else how that family is feeling.

Of all the thousands of Gold Rush diaries that survive, we remember those with vivid images, like the one by the captain of a ship coming around Cape Horn who told how he periodically came into the galley and leaned over the teapot to defrost his mustache. And in the stories about Irish famine, we remember those with striking, unexpected descriptions, like how the mouths of the peasants had turned green from eating grass.

Use Your Senses

The word *images* sounds like a word for a picture, but it's used to refer to all five senses: sight, hearing, smell, touch, and taste. Use them all:

```
SIGHT: the tiny brown splotch where a cookie has been
filched from the tray
HEARING: the high-pitched hum at Thanksgiving dinner
that turns out to be your father's hearing aid
SMELL: the musty odor of your grandmother's closet,
which smells of stale cigarette smoke, overpolished
leather, and long-neglected laundry
TOUCH: the kid next door, getting ready to cut your
hair, drawing an eyebrow pencil across your forehead to
mark where your bangs should end
TASTE: the baloney on Kilpatrick's bread with mayo that
never again tasted the way it did when you were a kid
```

Smell might be the most important sense of all in autobiographical writing. It unlocks the past. In fact it's great at taking you from present to past: I know that I smell exhaust from a passing Muni bus on Market Street in San Francisco and for an instant I am nine again, standing in front of the post office with my thin white socks already disappearing into my shoes, as the school bus whooshes up in a cloud of exhaust and wavy air.

I can use that flashback in writing as the first of a series of connected memories, intensely reexperienced more than remembered. Sven Birkerts, in *The Art of Time in Memoir*, pointed out that before Proust had his famous cookie epiphany, he spent much time exhaustively collecting the facts of his experience for a more straight-forward sort of book. Then:

> A single taste swamped him with charged-up sensations
> of childhood, and in the light of this visceral reac-
> tion, his earlier reaching for remembered experience
> seemed irrelevant. The vital past, the living past, he
> realized, could not be systemically excavated; it lay
> distilled in the very details that had not been groomed
> into submission.

Flannery O'Connor said it takes an appeal to at least three of your reader's five senses to make a scene real. "If you are deprived of more than two of your five senses," she said, "you almost aren't there." She referred to this example from Flaubert's *Madame Bovary*:

> She struck the keys with aplomb and ran from top to
> bottom of the keyboard without a break. Thus shaken
> up, the old instrument, whose strings buzzed, could be
> heard at the other end of the village when the windows
> were open, and often the bailiff's clerk, passing along
> the highroad, bareheaded and in list slippers, stopped
> to listen, his sheet of papers in his hand.

Instead of telling us that Madame Bovary was playing the piano, Flaubert gets strings buzzing, the piano shaking, and the camera moving past Bovary out the window and past the town to a bailiff's clerk who has stopped to listen.

How do we know a bailiff's clerk really did stop to listen? Because we know what he had on his feet. "It's always necessary to remember," said O'Connor, "that the writer is much less immediately concerned with grand ideas and bristling emotion than he is with putting list slippers on clerks."

Use your senses to re-create the moment, and you'll parachute your reader into your pages so completely that he won't hear his own phone ringing: he'll be too distracted by the porcelain clink of your mother's compact on a vanity in Kentucky in 1974.

A more modern example? Say you work for a big New York magazine. They send you to the Midwest to cover a concert, and you come back with an accurate, nicely punctuated story that says something like, "It was really hot and really loud at the concert." You would find yourself collecting images from the experience of landing on a Manhattan sidewalk with the pages of your opus settling in a picturesque heap all around you.

This is what Alec Wilkinson actually wrote in his *New Yorker* piece on a Midwest concert by Sophia Ramos, a glam rock singer from the South Bronx (with my own notes added in parentheses):

```
On this blistering day of sullen farm heat, the needle
on a thermometer worn on a string around the neck of
a white boy like a piece of jewelry reads a hundred
degrees. The expressions on the faces of the every-
where kids are flat and abstracted, as if they had just
been yelled at. (sight) The band they're listening to
is playing so loud that the sound stirs the surface of
a glass of water on a table in a room a hundred yards
away. (hearing) Three white boys wearing shorts and no
shirts stop Sophia, and one of them asks for an auto-
graph. He extends his arm and Sophia writes with a
black felt-tip marker on his biceps. (touch)
```

That's three, we're there. Wilkinson found those images because he looked for them; he went through that crowd hoping, consciously or not, to find a way to show how hot it was, how loud. That's why writers carry notebooks.

THE CRAFTY WRITER

Extend your images by adding appositions. *Apposing* means putting one thing beside another; an *apposition* is a word or group of words that add detail to the original. The italics below show appositions added to the original sentence:

"I moved back to Kansas *with its flat plains and harsh winters.*"

"Her apartment was messy, *tank tops hanging off the oven, pizza boxes stacked in the open bottom dresser drawer, a fuchsia bra wrapped around a lampshade and forgotten.*"

"Within fifteen minutes a new scent began to waft its way through the kitchen, *edging through the other, more pleasant odors like an impatient man pushing his way through a crowd.*"

try this

Stick to the *things* in the world—to the concrete. Write about where the chairs were in the room. Write about the empty pool, or the shoes your mother threw off the ferry. Or focus on an object—the potbellied stove or the picture dangling lopsidedly from a nail—and gradually enlarge the view to show you and others in the room.

We saw earlier that Frank McCourt, whose best-selling memoir *Angela's Ashes* helped set off the memoir craze, tried all his adult life to write about his childhood. He and his brother even had a stage play based on it in New York. We saw that it wasn't until he was sixty-six that he found the unjudging tone of a child that he needed to tell that horrific story.

McCourt found that tone through an ordinary object. It was during a classroom exercise at New York University, in which the students were asked to write about their childhood beds:

I wrote about the bed we slept in, we—my three brothers
and myself. It was a great half-acre of mattress with
red hair sticking out of it, no blankets, sheets, or
anything like that. And the professor said, "Oh, that's
vivid, would you read it to the class?" And I wouldn't,
because I was ashamed of my background, my poverty. But
I put it away, and I remembered what he said about how
vivid it was. I started writing little things, keeping
notes about growing up in Limerick.

Build Images with Specific Details

The terms "image" and "detail" are often used interchangeably. A concrete detail, for example, is said to be one that appeals to one of the five senses. I'm using the word "detail" here to refer to a particular and specific piece of information: "She wore a size 36C bra." Or, "My first car was a hot rod, a red Ford Fairlane with a 428 Cobrajet engine. It would go an astounding, whiplash-producing 3 m.p.h. when my college pals and I pushed it to the gas station for repair, which was 99 percent of the time."

Here's a passage from a piece by travel editor John Flinn that illustrates how to deftly insert details:

What started in 1912 with 122 sturdy young men huffing
from the Ferry Building to the Cliff House—and dodging
traffic along the way—has evolved into what it is today: 350 seeded and elite runners being pursued across
the city by a churning, panting sea of humanity looking
like a mass audition for a Village People reunion.

The details are "1912," "122," "Ferry Building," and "350 seeded and elite runners." We get that information in the midst of lively images, such as the conceit that the lead runners are being chased rather than leading.

If images let your reader experience what you experienced, then details prove it happened. If you say you are late because you hit traffic, the boss may compress his lips, but if you say some bozo in a MINI Cooper tried to drive along the margin of the road and hit a gravel truck, you have a shot at being believed. Want to convince us that your boyfriend's messy? Tell us you can write your name on the back of his toilet. If he's neat, say he aligns the pot handles on the stove. Don't tell the reader that your sister was artistic; say that "she painted the outside of her claw-foot tub like a Rousseau jungle, tacked postcards of Matisse and Klee paintings on the walls, walked around barefoot, and dyed her hair black."

You may be tempted not to bore the reader with the name of your elementary school or the name of the jeans you pined for. But put them in! Readers pounce on the smallest details. One woman wrote to me about an image I used in a piece, about people clicking by uncaring in their Nine Wests. "It's been bugging me," she said. "Don't you think the image would have worked better if you had said 'in their Pradas' or 'in their Clergeries'? 'Nine Wests' just seem so common, don't you think?"

The details also allow the readers to bring their own experiences to the page. Mention a Suzy Homemaker Oven and a female reader of a certain age will be rocketed back to the time when she was nine years old and cooking tiny pies with the heat of a lightbulb. This is one of the ways in which the reader participates in the story—by bringing her own associations to it.

THE BEST DETAILS COME FROM LIFE

My student Joan Murray wrote in a class essay, "If your protesting is serious, don't wear your Birkenstocks. Be sure to wear something with a reinforced toe so that you don't scrape your toes when you go limp and the police drag you away."

Has she really been to a protest at an abortion clinic? She sure as hell has. That detail proves it. Another student wrote, "Dad gave me the most inappropriate gifts for Christmas. When I was eleven, he gave me a deep-fat fryer, and at thirteen, it was a vacuum cleaner—

used." No way had this essayist made up the deep-fat fryer, right? That's what her father gave her. Another writer mentioned that after years as a masseuse she couldn't get a passport: Her fingerprints were too worn down. Who but a masseuse would know that?

What do you want to write about? Burning out yet another clutch, falling in love, raising a son? Whatever it is, it has been said before. Your challenge is to find a new way to say an old thing. For that, you need your wonderful voice and those cranky, eccentric details that could come only from a frontier where no one else has been: your life. You say what happened to you, using images and details that come directly from your experience, and magically your story is transformed into a story about the rest of us.

DETAILS, YES, BUT WHICH DETAILS?

In the first draft, put them all in. Later, pare down to the significant, the surprising, and the fresh observation. Sometimes less is more: The impressionistically rendered scene tends to hit us harder than the one photo realistically reported. This is because we fill in the rest from our imaginations and thus participate in the writing. A photographer for the *New York Times* said, "When you stand in Baghdad with the sand under your feet, you're in the middle of a civil war." What better image to show a city breaking up, returning to desert under the destructive force of battling factions? You don't have to add the block after block of collapsed buildings—they're implied.

A coffee cup being rinsed will give us the kitchen; a glance at a bedroom clock, the bedroom; a dying geranium, the deck. A Japanese painting shows you a cherry branch and you have the whole tree in glorious bloom.

You develop a sense, in time, for what the reader needs to know, and what he doesn't. In the meantime, whatever you do, don't delete the weird stuff. You think that cream of mushroom soup's aftertaste resembles the taste of Cap'n Crunch cereal? Tell us. You like the drool spots on a cool pillow? We want to hear that.

The most neurotic details resonate like a tuning fork. Who could forget the story about a jealous astronaut driving from Texas to New

York to intercept her lover's new girlfriend—and wearing a diaper so she wouldn't have to stop to pee? A *diaper*! During the 2008 Super Bowl, bananas were rushed to the bench after a coach decided the players needed more potassium. "There are the bananas," the announcer said, as if we home viewers could not pick them out. Of course we could: We were riveted by seeing bananas appearing in a championship football game. It was the kind of weird detail you notice.

THE CRAFTY WRITER

Even when you need a lot of detail, as in a longer piece or a book, feed it to us a little at a time rather than (as someone or other put it) in one great lump. This is especially true when you're introducing people in your narrative. Don't give us a great block of text that we will have to thumb back to when we are finally interested in Aunt Betty. Add a bit of information about her with each fresh appearance.

USE DETAILS TO LOCATE US IN TIME AND SPACE

A man who warms Dinty Moore stew on the radiator of a '54 Olds has a different lifestyle than a man spooning up beef bourguignon at the Paris Ritz. The fan of *Bonanza* reruns is different from the *Antiques Roadshow* enthusiast. You can give us the era by telling us what song is playing on the radio: "'Sugar. Ah, honey, honey. You are my candy girl . . .' sang the Archies over and over the summer I was seven."

My student Rita Hargrave wrote an essay about her experience the day after Dr. Martin Luther King, Jr., was shot dead in Memphis, Tennessee:

> The year was 1968. My father and I were going to see
> *My Fair Lady* again, and my head was already full of
> the song "On the Street Where You Live." I didn't no-
> tice how my father avoided my eyes, nor that he was
> so distracted that we rolled through a red light. As
> we sped north on 16th Street, I did notice that the

streets were oddly deserted for two in the afternoon.
I glanced at my father. He was frowning, chewing his
lower lip and staring ahead as we rounded Logan Circle
and passed the darkened yellow neon sign of People's
Drug Store, one of the city's few twenty-four-hour
drugstores. It was closed, the lights off. There was
no sign of the hordes of mahogany-colored teenagers—
Catholic school girls in white blouses and navy pleated
skirts—who gathered there every afternoon, squealing,
shouting, and wolfing down fistfuls of Lay's potato
chips. Logan was the dividing line. Past it the neighborhood got meaner, dotted with crumbling rowhouses
with patchy lawns, raucous storefront churches, and
shoeshine parlors.

Notice all the details of place and time that ground us here, adding to the tension and proving that this is a real experience. We get
"speeding north on 16th Street" as opposed to "drove across town."
We get the disquieting sight of the darkened yellow neon sign of the
usually busy People's Drug Store.

Don't give us a box of cereal, but a box of Wheaties. Not a tree,
but an aspen. A car didn't pull into your space: a green MINI Cooper
did. A certain ex-president's affectionate intern wore not just lipstick
but Club Monaco Glaze lipstick and Club Monaco Bare lip liner.
"Adopted a tabby from outside a darkened Walmart storefront," is
better than "brought home a stray cat."

Notice the names in this passage from my writing partner Marsh
Rose's piece about being a drug therapist in a county jail:

Tammi Lynn could have gotten her tattoo in only one
place in town. Donatello's Skin Design was on the lower
end of the main drag, between a Harley-Davidson chopper
shop and an adult bookstore. I elbowed my way past the
small group thumbing through a rack of catalogs, past a
silver-haired executive type in a Tarzan T-shirt with

> a young thing in black leather plastered to his side.
> I saw the two problem children of Doreen O'Reilly, the
> Dolly Parton wannabe checker down at Tiny's Market.

Notice how much more interesting this is than, "There was a tattoo shop on the lower end of the main drag. I walked in." (Of course, if the tattoo shop was not important, this would be too much detail.)

GIVE EXAMPLES

It's okay to make an assertion, but follow it up with the proof. When you tell me your boyfriend is cheap, tell me how you know—perhaps that he stopped at a water fountain when you said you wanted a drink, and bought a car without a radio.

> ASSERTION: My grandmother tried to hide the evidence of
> her marital problems.
> EXAMPLE: Every morning the covers on the twin bed in
> the spare bedroom were smoothed and tucked and flat-
> tened with precision, even if she had just risen.
>
> ASSERTION: I didn't come from a drinking family.
> EXAMPLE: For twenty years, my father saved the annual
> bottle of scotch he was given at Christmas for my older
> sister Marcia's wedding day. When that day came and she
> married an Englishman, he distributed the booze frugal-
> ly, exactly one bottle per table of twelve.

If you say, "I had to help my mother when she started dating," we have an unsubstantiated assertion. Give us examples, as my student Kathryn Kefauver did when she said, "At home I showed my mother how to control the spray-pump on her Chanel No. 5, to fluff her hair with a round brush, and to purge her speech of terms like 'necking' and 'going steady.'" (Notice that Kathryn gives three examples—for some reason, humans like examples that come in threes.)

The Dread Necessity of Inner Emotional Landscape

An essay, like a memoir, is an emotional story. Here's the rule: If there is no emotion in the narrator, there will be none in the reader. You say your house burned down, taking with it your childhood photo albums and Steinway piano. If you don't feel anything, we don't feel anything. A story is nothing more than images with feelings attached. Jonathan Safran Foer, author of *Everything Is Illuminated*, said that for him the key to good writing was, "Let me slow down and tell you exactly what I'm feeling."

Have you ever noticed that in movies, every action is followed by a shot of someone's face, registering a reaction? Even in a televised basketball game, every time something happens—a muffed shot, a foul, a score, a missed free throw—the camera moves to the coach so we can see his expression. He frowns, or talks excitedly into his headpiece, and we are satisfied. In a football game, it's not enough to see the fumble, the football loose on the grass: We have to see somebody react. Those feelings and reaction shots are called the *inner emotional landscape*.

So, how to show feelings? You can certainly state them directly: "I was angry." Or, even better, suggest them: "I spat my toothpaste right where I knew my husband wanted to spit his."

It did not come naturally to me, this business of learning to put in feelings. I was like the late columnist Molly Ivins, who said, "I tend to treat my emotions like unpleasant relatives—a long-distance call once or twice a year is more than enough." When my agent sent several chapters of *Hold Me Close, Let Me Go* to New York, many of the editors who read it said they wanted more "inner emotional landscape." Even before the editors saw the manuscript, other readers missed evidence of feeling. My friend Wendy Lichtman, who was in my writing group when I worked on that memoir, had a teenage daughter herself. She'd stir impatiently as I read my pages aloud about allowing sixteen-year-old Morgan's boyfriend to sleep over. "What's the mother feeling when that happens?" she wanted to know.

I thought it was enough to say what my hell-child was doing—skipping out of the house when she was already grounded, say—for readers to know how I felt. It seemed unsubtle to spell it out. But I had to learn to think like an actor: What do I feel in my body when I'm sad or worried or joyful? How can I express those feelings through action? It's like method acting, only you're playing yourself, making those interior feelings visible to an imagined audience beyond the footlights.

Here's what I came up with to show what I felt when the boy slept over:

```
We all went to bed, exhausted from the move. Some of
us anyway: I kept hearing loud sounds of lovemaking
coming from the room next to mine, groaning and bed-
springs, and then a bed banging against the wall, and
laughter. I found a pair of earplugs in my dresser
drawer, stuffed a pillow over my head. Still, the
sounds penetrated, and I comforted myself by imagining
her hanging out on some street in another city, ask-
ing passersby for cash, her unwashed hair stringy on
her pale forehead. I imagined her sitting beside a car
on a deserted road with her head in her hands, bloody
from a car wreck. I thought of my niece Erin, off in
Texas somewhere.
       She was not any of those things. She was warm and
dry and safe, and, from the sound of it, happy.
```

USE DESCRIPTION TO REVEAL EMOTION

As the poet Stephane Mallarme said, "Paint not the thing, but the effect which it produces." A child's train left out on the rug can bring a fond smile or a surge of exasperation. You can show tenderness or impatience in the act of brushing an insect from a child's mosquito netting.

What you notice, and what you don't, also conveys feeling. If you describe a house as having surfaces cluttered with knickknacks and an endlessly barking dog, we know that you don't want to be there.

In a draft of a memoir about her anorexic daughter, my student Casey Simon relates how she sent her child to a psychiatric hospital. We know how she feels about the place from her description of it:

> It was a big brick building that I had walked past many
> times on my way to the nearby medical center. I had
> never been inside, but I'd pictured what went on behind
> the big double doors, behind the overgrown pine shrubs
> that seemed to be wrestling for dominance with the ag-
> gressive ice plant chewing up the front lawn. Even the
> big oak tree in front of the hospital looked gnarled
> and twisted, more sinister than the oaks in front of
> the buildings on either side.

In *Tiger's Eye*, Inga Clendinnen reveals how she felt stripped of dignity during a hospital stay by describing her gown:

> Social trappings are surrendered along with clothes
> and other valuables at the door of the ward. Abruptly
> naked, you are thrust into a vestigial smock. Starched,
> snowy, it rises high to the chin, but stops, incredi-
> bly, at the crotch, and at the back the little ties end
> with the rib cage. When you move, your buttocks show.
> It is at once lewd and sexless. An outfit designed for
> depraved choirboys. When you climb into the bed the
> bottom sheet strikes cold on bare skin, you feel thick
> tucked stuff under you, and chill with forgotten shame:
> rubber sheeting.

Let's look at my student Kat Brennan's memory of her parents on the beach:

> When my father bent forward to let her get his back,
> his gray-furred chest collapsed on his belly. He looked
> old and soft. He had on the felt hat he always wore at

the lake, the one with the speckly quail feather tucked
in its band. Mom capped the Coppertone, sat back down
in her stubby plastic-webbed beach chair, and took a
swallow from her gin-and-tonic. Her short, bleached-
blond curls were so stiff with hairspray they remained
rigid even in the wind that puffed up off the lake's
surface. She might have been happy or sad or angry behind her sunglasses.

Notice how the details tell us what the narrator is feeling: This
is a vulnerable dad, his "gray-furred chest collapsed on his belly," one
who might not be around forever. Is Mom sad and vulnerable? No.
The tension builds. Later the choice of verbs add to the bleak feeling we get—waves *slap*, a brother *stumbles* along the shore, his swim
trunks *sag*, the minnows *spin* in furious circles. Every image does
much more than paint the scene: it adds emotional complexity and
foreboding.

try this

- Write about the thing beside the thing—the shoe in the gutter
  near the burned-out apartment buildings. A friend of mine,
  Karen Thomas, wrote about death and family, and said, "The
  smallest things took on importance, and the periphery moved
  center stage as if the main event could not be approached or
  maybe was too big to get on the page. I wrote the main event,
  so to speak, but it was clouded or cushioned by details that
  were as vivid as the death itself."

- Look over a piece of yours and rewrite a sentence, adding
  detail and image. My student Jean Shiffman's original was,
  "On trips, my mother reads, which she always does anyway
  at home, and my father drives." Her rewrite: "On trips, my
  mother reads Agatha Christie novels one after the other,
  leaving the finished books behind in motel rooms for other

kindred spirits. My father drives silently. My mother says he is thinking of mathematical formulas in his head."

- Write a page each on the themes of:
    My mother's drawer
    My father's tools
    My father's house
    My mother's hands

So let's say you've thought of all kinds of wonderful images and jotted down intriguing details. But there's still one tiny problem: You have yet to write any of those images, details, or ideas on paper or computer screen. Your images and ideas are just that—images and ideas floating around in the ether of your mind. How do you get yourself to write them down, especially when you're not ready or you're too busy or you're lazy or, worst of all, you're scared? The answer to that question is the subject of the next chapter.

HOW TO
TRICK YOURSELF
INTO WRITING

I write when I'm inspired, and I see to it that
I'm inspired at nine o'clock every morning.

—PETER DE VRIES

Oh, boy. So much to think about, right? I've spent years learning and teaching this stuff, and here I am throwing it at you all at once. If I were you, I'd be feeling overwhelmed, like one of my students, Hank Martinson, who emailed me after one class to say:

> Yesterday morning, as I was happily cranking out material,
> I was thinking, "It's about time I got an agent." This
> morning, after class last night, all I can think is,
> "It's about time I got an angle." An *angle*! Son of a
> bitch! Who even knew about an *angle*?

So let's take a break from craft and talk instead about ways to get your reluctant little self sitting down at the desk in the first place. It seems so simple: The job of a writer is to put words on paper. You have paper and a pen, or a laptop. You have a good light and a chair. You want to write and often feel that you *must* write. So write! Go ahead!

I know. Writing is scary. It turns your skin inside out. I know that if I even think about writing, I find myself in the pantry eating Honey Nut Cheerios straight from the box. When I travel I always lose weight, because when I'm not writing, I'm not nervous. My friend Wendy Lichtman says writing can make her feel sick to the point that she wonders if it's the chemical fumes from the carpet. As *Feast of Love* author Charles Baxter observed, "Bracing self-confidence among writers is a rare commodity and often a sign of psychic instability." I think he might be right: an editor friend of mine told me his company's best-selling book on phobias lacked an author photo because the author couldn't stand having his picture taken.

And there's all that good writing out there. I know I was blocked for years by the chasm between what others wrote and what I scrawled in my notebook. I'd write, "I wish I could set things down the way I see them in my head." Then I'd read Flaubert's version of the same thought: "Human language is like a cracked kettle on which we beat out tunes for bears to dance to, when all the time we are longing to move the stars to pity."

I had the cracked kettle—he had the stars weeping.

No one is free of doubts, no matter how much success they've had:

> Can I write? Will I write if I practice enough? How much should I sacrifice to writing anyway, before I find out if I'm any good? Above all, CAN A SELFISH EGO-CENTRIC JEALOUS AND UNIMAGINATIVE FEMALE WRITE A DAMN THING WORTHWHILE?

If you're wondering who stole that thought out of your head, it was Sylvia Plath. And she already knew her poems pierced the skin.

Apply Part A (Butt) to Part B (Chair)

The will to not write is strong in all of us. That's not going to stop being true, so you need to tiptoe around it by changing your approach. To start off, give yourself ridiculously easy goals that have nothing to do with writing well or publishing. Don't vow to write. Vow to show up at the desk. Forget trying to write well, and instead go for a certain number of words a day. (Some writers log how many words they write each day on the calendar, to keep themselves honest.) Switch your aim from getting published to, say, collecting rejection slips until you can paper the bathroom with them.

STEP ONE: PICK A SPOT AND SHOW UP

Let's start by having you show up regularly at a place where writing can occur. Get in the habit of sitting down at the same place at the same time in order to write. If you don't have a habit, you have to decide all over again every day to write. And how many times will the answer be yes?

They say it takes three weeks to form a habit. Force yourself for that long to stick to your routine. Let's say that you choose to write at your desk for twenty minutes at 6:30 a.m. Every morning, march your pajama-clad self from your warm bed to the desk at the agreed-on time.

Don't require yourself to do any actual writing just yet. You can clean out your junk drawer, play solitaire, draw caricatures of your ex-boyfriends, go through your pens and throw out the ones that don't work. If you feel like doing a little writing as long as you're there, that's fine, but the important thing is not the writing. It's the showing up. After awhile, you won't have to force yourself.

Your designated writing spot doesn't have to be in your house. It could also be in the library, a coffee shop, or the park. If you do want to write at home, don't feel confined to traditional work spaces either—set up a card table in the hall or curl up in the front seat of your car. Any place that has *no Internet or phone*, no whites to be separated from colors, and no vintage family pictures in emergency need of reframing. Flannery O'Connor sat at the typewriter for two hours every day, facing the back of her clothes dresser so she would have nothing to look at to distract her. (She probably knew if she let herself look at the front of the dresser she'd spend the day rearranging her socks or painting bunnies on it.)

STEP TWO: EASE INTO WRITING

Once sitting down to write becomes a second-nature routine rather than a dreaded chore, slowly ease yourself into the process. If you go to the coffee house, bring a yellow legal pad and a nice pen, order a large latte, and write for thirty minutes on why you left home. Did your friend in the antipodes send you a yellow Panama hat? Write about that. Your husband's away and you miss him, or your friend Rosalie's in Rome, drinking too much red wine in trattorias? Start there. If you need some inspirational prompts to get the juices flowing, try an exercise in the appendix (pages 232–241).

No email monitoring during your writing period! No poring over home-exchange sites—"that darling bungalow in Provence, I must email this to my husband . . ." What if Thomas Jefferson had had email? He wouldn't have gotten anything done! He'd have been too busy clicking on links and instant messaging Sally What's-Her-Name.

STEP THREE: STICK TO THE SCHEDULE

Show up on a fixed schedule. Deborah Santana, who lives in San Rafael over the Golden Gate Bridge from me, wrote her writing times on the family calendar—"2-5 Deborah at Dominican College Library"—so her husband would, ahem, get over his evil ways and take them seriously. Or maybe it was so that *she* would take them seriously. In any event, now she has a published memoir, *Space Between the Stars*.

INDULGE YOURSELF A LITTLE BEFORE SETTLING DOWN

I'd like to say I settle into my chair and start turning out prose with great concentration, but it isn't like that. I sneak out of my office to weep over the last ten minutes of the movie *Parenthood*, have another piece of the low-carb bread that my husband gets from somewhere on the Internet, and leaf through catalogs (after a few months of working at home, $159 doesn't seem like too much for a plug-in wall hair dryer). Don't be too strict. Give yourself a half hour of party time before you settle down.

THE CRAFTY WRITER

Develop your own prewriting ritual. It can be as quirky and out there as you want, as long as it's legal in forty-eight states, gets you in a creative mood, and ends with you at the desk. So go ahead, make the bed, put on your special writing fleece, throw the Frisbee for the dog. Strut around the house in librarian glasses and four-inch red pumps.

Professional writers have their own inspiring routines. British novelist Hilary Mantel, author of *Wolf Hall*, sits down to write first thing in the morning—before she says a word and even before she has her coffee. Nicholson Baker gets up at 4 a.m. and writes for two hours with the computer screen turned to black. Junot Diaz, author of *The Brief Wondrous Life of Oscar Wao*, listens to orchestral soundtracks as he writes. Richard Powers lies in bed and dictates his novels to his laptop through a microphone.

WHAT NOT TO WORRY ABOUT WHEN YOU SIT DOWN TO WRITE

Is it any good?

Is it too short or too long?

Why would anybody care about this?

What if somebody reads it?

What if nobody does?

WHAT YOU *SHOULD* WORRY ABOUT

Did I write today?

Write Every Day

Challenge yourself to write every day. Sound impossible? It sure does, but it's not. A few years back Pulitzer Prize-winning poet Suzan-Lori Parks, author of *Topdog/Underdog*, decided to write a play a day for a year. The subject matter for these exercises, most only a few pages long, ranged from deities to soldiers to what she saw out of her plane window. Afterward those plays were produced all over the country at the same time, but that's not the point. The point is she came up with a way to make herself produce new work every day. I also heard of an inventor who refused to let himself get out of bed on Saturday mornings until he'd thought up something new.

A poet named David Lehman did the same when he challenged himself to write a poem a day. "Writing a poem every day for several years will diminish the preciosity of your writing," he said. "You find yourself willing to write about things that don't seem obviously poetical." Not a problem for the rest of us, perhaps (the being obviously poetical thing), but you get his point.

Try not to skip. Until you get on the talk shows and your name appears on checks, acting like a writer is the only way to know you are one. If you don't write on Monday, you will feel less like a writer on Tuesday. By Wednesday, you might be feel so guilty that you throw a sweater over the laptop. By Thursday, you will be certain that taking the Honda in to get that unraveling strip of rubber glued down is a better use of your time than pretending you're a writer.

Most professional writers write every day. Ayn Rand, author of *Atlas Shrugged*, said she regarded the blank sheet of paper in front of her as her employer. She had to fill it. "If you do not regard writing as a job," she said, "self-doubt will necessarily enter your mind, and you will be paralyzed." (You can go one step further in making that sheet of paper your employer if you pay yourself for writing, so much for so many words. Why not? Whatever works.)

These days, a blog makes a good daily exercise. Many books have begun as daily blogs, like that one by a woman who cooked something different every day for a year, and another one by a woman who accompanied her husband to Bosnia and wrote home to her email list. (I consider an email list as a kind of blog.)

Writing every day will give you a stack of material. But that's not all it will do. It will also give you license to dream. If you go to the library at lunchtime every day and write, you can while away those dull regional sales meetings thinking about the book, planning your slinky black outfit for the publication party, making lists of whom to thank as you accept the National Book Award, practicing your signature for book readings. It also means that you'll carry your ideas around in your head for the rest of the day. You'll be writing as you hand a clerk a burned-out lightbulb or toss the junk mail or deadhead the daisies or fire that useless junior partner. There you'll be, waiting in line at Best Buy to return your iPod speakers, the strap of your purse digging into your shoulder, and you'll realize that if you start the piece with the day your husband insisted on buying the loud yellow canary, it will flow better.

No Time to Write? Consider Yourself Lucky

You have a full-time job? Thirty-eight-year-old Khaled Hosseini rose at 5 a.m. to write, at first short stories, then a novel, until it was time to go to thump on chests and squeeze tummies as an internist. That's how he became the author of his first book, *The Kite Runner*, the hugely best-selling novel of an Afghan immigrant's return to Kabul.

I heard that the writer Rumer Godden wrote many of her books in five-minute sessions between all sorts of terrible things happening (cobras attacking her children in the highlands of Kashmir, that sort of thing). And you have to do what, again? Return phone calls? Pay bills? Work all day and then feed the kids and put them to bed? As Robyn Carr pointed out in a *Writer's Digest* article, "There are hardly any writers, outside of the federal penitentiary, who got started because they had time to kill."

Ayn Rand, that model of indefatigableness, claimed that she accepted no daytime or evening appointments for thirteen years while writing *Atlas Shrugged*. (She probably had no friends by then, but still. All those books.)

Having all the time in the world to write can be paralyzing. In one episode of the sitcom *Roseanne*, the star told her husband, Dan, "It's always been my dream to write children's books." Dan promptly cleared out the basement. He brought in an old wooden desk and plunked a typewriter, pencils, and a stack of blank paper on it. "Now you can write!" he beamed as he and the kids tiptoed away.

Next shot: Roseanne in the basement sitting in front of an untouched stack of blank paper with a panicked expression. It was as if the world said, "So, you're a writer, are you? Go ahead. Write." And then the world watched, sneering, arms folded. Roseanne had a place to write, a time to write. Freed from little anxieties, she was ready to be overwhelmed by larger ones, such as having no ideas or talent. The same thing can happen when people go on sabbatical to write or set aside an entire expansive retirement for that task. Wait! I was kidding! *Guys, don't leave me here with this ream of paper! Guys . . .*

Lower Your Standards

Know how Tom Wolfe got started? He was writing a story on a hot rod and custom car show in California for *Esquire* magazine when he found himself blocked. He knew how magazine pieces were written, and his wasn't coming out right no matter how many times he crumpled up the page and started over.

He gave up. He called his editor, Byron Dobell, and Dobell said, well, okay, just type up your notes and send them over.

So Wolfe started typing at about 8 p.m. in the form of a memo that began, "Dear Byron." He started with the first time he saw the custom cars. Freed of any need to plan the piece properly, he typed like a madman. All night. At 6:15 a.m., he took the 49-page memo over to *Esquire*.

At 4 p.m., Dobell called to say he was taking off the "Dear Byron" and running the rest in the magazine.

That became *The Kandy-Kolored Tangerine Flake Streamlined Baby*, a benchmark in journalism. Wolfe had found his voice by letting the writing flow out however it wanted to.

Forget trying to produce good writing.

Think it stinks? Make it worse on purpose. Another way in: Pretend no one will read it. Pretend you're jotting down notes for a piece, not, good heavens, composing the piece itself. Force your fingers to peck on without worrying about whether you're just whining on the page or whether that last sentence is a train wreck and whether *train wreck* is exactly a fresh expression.

Write a letter. My friend Joan Frank once started a letter to a friend about the experience of turning forty. About midway through, it dawned on her (the way the euphoric caveman understood his new power, tossing a bone in the air in the film *2001*) that if she cut off "Dear Maria" and "Love, Joan" she was staring at her very first essay. Shortly thereafter, the piece was accepted by *The Utne Reader*.

Or set a kitchen timer. Writing often feels like a duty—*I'm supposed to be writing!* A timer means you have to write only until the bell rings. My student Cecilia Worth described what it's like for her to write in such short timed bursts:

```
I do not stop for a minimum of fifteen minutes. What
I have found is that it will be weird and superficial
for a while, and suddenly, like breaking through a long
cloudy airplane run and seeing the green field below,
I consciously put off the voice that tells me to stop
because I have to go to the store, to phone, to lay off
because the topic is garbage. Sort of like I'm waving
it off, while writing furiously, saying, wait, wait, I
just have to finish this. This is certainly not a new
exercise, but it works every time for me. I believe
that doing it impresses my subconscious that writing
is indeed a priority. Once I did this every day at
```

```
the same time for three months, at the end of which my
piece on a patient with HIV was published in the Sunday
New York Times Magazine.
```

Being stuck does not always mean that you are out of ideas. It can mean that you're getting to the heart of things, which is scary, so you stop. I've noticed that overly fluent writers, those to whom words come fast, have trouble going deep in their writing: Sometimes you need that block, that thing that stops you. In fact, some writers feel comforted when they get stuck, because they know from experience it's a sign they're now inside the project with both feet.

If in the middle of your story you don't remember what happened next or don't know what else to write, stop, walk around, and transport yourself back to the place you were writing about. Feel what it's like to be in that room, absorb what you see around you, notice who is there with you and who isn't. Then start writing again.

All of the above methods will help you get words on paper. For me, though, the best way to get myself to produce a lot of new writing—and get some encouragement and constructive advice at the same time—is to get myself into a room (or at least into an email exchange) with other writers. So now that you know how to trick yourself into writing, let's look in the next chapter at how you keep writing with the help of your writing friends.

eight

IT TAKES A VILLAGE
Working with Other Writers

The worst of writing is that one depends so much upon praise.

—VIRGINIA WOOLF

I F YOU remember, I started this book by talking about my first writing partnership, with Cynthia who worked for the same city magazine that I did. Cynthia's clear voice drowned out my hectoring inner critic, allowing me, at last, to embark on a writing career.

I had another writing partner later, called Nini. She wrote about her job at *Screw* magazine and about family drinking (including family-owned drunk tanks) that make my family look like teetotalers. She wrote about her shar-pei, about Southern women, about her dad, about one-night stands ("one-night tilts, really"), about adult children of alcoholics meetings, about spray painting "The Incredible John Ceneca" in blue enamel through a stencil onto her boyfriend's chest. She wrote about her house: "There are times I fear, looking at this huge house, that in fact I am married and have children (for what else could explain this place?) but that they have temporarily slipped my mind."

In turn, I wrote about a man I was trying to get into bed, about kids, about my family, about escaping turtles, about dying my hair orange, about the thieves who came in the night and stole the new blue fur seat cover on my Toyota after I had left the sunroof open. I loved having a writing partner again. Having a captive reader—someone who will cheerfully read any drivel you care to write—is such a lovely, rewarding experience that I highly recommend this to you: Find other writers to exchange work with. When I don't have a writing partner or a writing group, I bog down, go in circles, or endlessly rewrite. Over the years, my writing partners have been like people with flashlights on a dark highway. They tell me which roads not to take, when to speed up, when to slow down. They are objective—they see what's on the page, whereas I see what I thought I wrote. They ask good questions. When I'm discouraged, they say, "It's fabulous, just keep going!"

How Writing Partners Make You Write

When I was hired by the *San Francisco Chronicle*, it was on the strength of ten sample columns—which I had on hand only because of my exchanges with my first two writing partners, Cynthia and Nini.

Once I'd been given the ID card that let me into the newspaper building, though, I naturally assumed I didn't need anything as amateurish as writing partners anymore. I was a professional! It said "writer" on my income tax return. I had the paper to give me deadlines: every Tuesday at 4 p.m. and every Thursday at 4 p.m.

Five years went by. I'd written about everything I could think of, from seeing a shrink at the behest of a boyfriend to the slow days of summer to book clubs. I'd start a piece about finding spare change in the couch and then remember I'd already written about that. I was so played out that I envied the people at bus stops, who were heading to jobs where people told them what to do. I scrawled "Writing is fun!" on my computer with a Sharpie, to remind myself, but I didn't believe it. The newspaper guild allowed a sabbatical after five years, and the day I was eligible I took six months' unpaid leave. I was convinced this was just stalling: I would not be returning to the paper.

That first Monday of my sabbatical, I turned off the computer. I helped my son, Patrick, with his Mongol report, drove my daughter, Morgan, to the DMV for her learner's permit, taught the dog to play hide and seek, and replaced the batteries in all three of our remotes.

I had begun teaching by this time, and one day Ginny McReynolds, a former student, appeared in my kitchen with a wild plan about driving down from Sacramento once a month, bringing two essays and lunch. She was my age, with short brown-gray hair and wide blue eyes. Ginny was on sabbatical herself from her job advising the school paper for Sacramento City College. "How about if we start a long-distance writing club instead?" I suggested. We agreed to mail each other our writing and then send back our marked-up pieces.

The first requisite of a writing partner is steadiness. Ginny was steady. If they bombed the Sacramento post office, the TV news would show one determined woman picking her way among the dust and rubble, bent on mailing her letter to San Francisco.

Three months later, as the stack of pieces marked with Ginny's yellow highlighting rose on my desk, I went back to work early. I figured that if I was doing all this writing, I should be getting paid for it. I quit trying to write a column and started writing to Ginny every day. When she liked something, I'd put it in the paper. The years flew by on a surge of renewed energy.

I'd remembered, again, how important it is to change the goal. I'd begun to find it paralyzing to write for an audience of 300,000 readers. But writing to Ginny? That was easy.

Since then I've tried always to have a writing partner—another person to exchange writing with, several days a week. Right now, as I write this, I'm swamped: I'm meeting a new class tonight, I have damp grandtots to ferry to school because their mother has an early morning court appearance, and I'm behind on two manuscripts I'm reviewing. It seems like a crazy time to worry about doing my daily writing, but in my experience this is when it matters most to keep it up: when life gets crazy. Certainly my present writing partner understands this: I get emails that she dashed off late at night in a hotel room after a long business day. The email will say something like "This is all I could do today"—but there it is, that little paper clip in my email, the daily exercise that is life's breath to a writing partnership.

How the Writing Partnership Works

It's pretty simple. Once you have a writing partner, you will either meet in person or, more commonly, exchange work by email on an agreed-on schedule. (I used to do it by regular mail, waiting eagerly for the post each day.) When you get your partner's emailed piece, just open the email and hit Reply. Now you can type in comments. Use all caps so it's easy for your partner to tell your comments from her prose. I use the word *NICE* in place of yellow highlighting.

You can also send the exercise as an attachment, if your computers are compatible. The advantage is that you can open the attachment in, say, Microsoft Word, which has a cool option under Tools called Track Changes. You turn it on and can make all sorts of suggestions without wiping out the original document.

I realize that many (male) writers sniff at the idea of showing their words to anyone. This is how male writers operate: *I am man. I will go into jungle and write book.* My friend Jeremy is an example. He worked on a novel for five years. He took only as much engineering work as he had to in order to pay the bills and showed the book to no one but his wife. Then he UPS'ed the manuscript to me (and to other friends), bought me a Caesar salad at the Grind around the corner on Haight Street, and asked me what I thought of it. "It's great," I said. It was actually confusing and repetitious—but what else could I say? At that stage in the process, he was asking for praise, not suggestions. His book was self-published years later.

Once I interviewed Don DeLillo in his shadowy room in the Four Seasons hotel on Market Street about his latest book, *Cosmopolis*. He said he had not shown it to his wife or anybody but his agent and his editor (and I got the feeling he really would have preferred not to show it to them). All during the interview I was thinking what an awful book *Cosmopolis* was, and what I really wanted to ask was, "Jesus, Don, have you no friends? No one to say, 'You know, Don . . .'?"

Yes, I know. We girl writers write a paragraph and nervously email it to ten people before going on. We seek so much feedback that we end up confused by contradictory advice and unpracticed in relying on our instincts. Even Rosellen Brown, author of *Before and After*, said, "While I'm a decent critic of a word or a line of my own, I have little faith in my capacity to judge the whole, at least until a great deal of time goes by and possibly not even then."

And yes, I know I'm making huge generalizations. Lots of men have taken my class, and I know women who (literally) work in closets and show their work to no one.

Still. Writing partners changed my life in powerful, simple ways: I am hardly likely to shut up about them anytime soon.

HOW TO FIND A WRITING PARTNER

The best way I know of, outside of asking friends or trying to get into a writing group, is to take a class and find your partners there. You want to find someone who is about your speed, so that one of you is not functioning as the teacher, the other as student. You will probably have several writing partners before you find the one for you. Things can go wrong for a lot of reasons—she'll pick at your grammar or give you blanket praise or just not get you, or vice versa.

KEEP IT RECIPROCAL

By the way, if one of you says, "Oh, I don't have time right now, but go ahead and send me your stuff," it stops working. *It must be reciprocal.* That is the other value of the right writing partner: You're in it together. Your partner is not just rubbernecking an accident as she passes by. She should be both the paramedic and on the stretcher next to you, breathing life into your work and exposing her own at the same time.

Also, if your writing club is to succeed, a writing partner must respond in the agreed-on time span (usually within a day). Otherwise you are right back where you started—staggering into the kitchen in your robe and vowing, "I will get some words down on paper today." And then you spend two hours updating Facebook and decide that you don't have time to write, but you will make it up by writing four hours tomorrow, and tomorrow brings a long boozy lunch with a college friend—and so it goes.

In my experience this is when it matters most to keep it up. Writing doesn't wait. Write in the good times and in the bad, and when nothing seems worth writing about at all.

You're busy. You see your partner's email with its attachment, but you have to find your son's soccer cleats among the sodden belongings in the trunk of your car, chase down the cat and give him his anti-flea medicine, and get water boiling for pasta. But reading a partner's email takes only fifteen minutes, and if you do it, you get all the wonderful things a good partnership can give you.

In every class I teach, I pair off students with each other (everybody gets a new partner every week) and give them assignments. Kathy Briccetti-Clark was one of them, and she published a piece in *Writers' Journal* in which she said:

> I was paired with a writing partner, someone to whom
> I promised that I would send 500 words a day ("Any
> 500 words: new, old, copied from the cereal box," our
> instructor told us.) For three weeks, I did write
> 500 words a day, and one time I wrote 2500 words in
> one sitting because I couldn't stop.
>
> I was getting into the habit. I was thinking of myself as a writer who happened to have a little side job
> outside the house. I began to sell my work. Last month
> I published a story about how we push aside our long-loved dogs when we have children, and my vet read it
> and said it made him want to go home and hug his dog. I
> saw a friend wipe her eyes when she read it.

Having a writing partner helped Kathy not only write but also get published. Very simple lesson here: nothing written, nothing published.

Take Classes

Unless you get an instructor who seems to hate writing (yours in particular) and loathe writing students (you in particular), almost any class you take is worth it. My students take my class again and again, not because I'm so freaking brilliant or because they like crossing bridges in the dark at night. They take it because when they're not in a class, they stop writing.

I hold my classes at the flat I share with my husband, Bill, in San Francisco, which is geographically right in the center of town; I once read that the city's temperature readings are taken at Duboce Park up the street from us. (I always wanted to find the thermometer and breathe on it.) Our living room has white shutters over the bay windows and the usual tiny Victorian fireplace at one end, along with an ever-changing collection of motley couches and chairs. Bill, a cookbook editor, goes out on class nights. I know he's home when I notice people unobtrusively pulling on their jackets and sweaters—it means he's turned off the heat.

For two and a half hours my students sit in there, squished next to one another on the two couches, or in folding chairs or on the floor. They tell their stories, teasing sense out of them, making them into art. Underneath their sweatshirts and suits burn inner lives brighter and more vital than their daytime lives.

These students might be the same ones who passed notes in biology class and refused to read *Ivanhoe*, thinking that education was an evil plot to make their lives miserable. Now they're piranhas waiting to be fed. They've paid for the class, have engaged babysitters, and have arranged time off work. I don't have to hear the restless shifting of their feet to know what they're feeling. They want me to change their lives.

Linda Robinson, who had breast cancer, came to classes at my house knowing she had less than a year to live. She was thirty-six, with thick blonde hair just growing in again, married, and living with two small sons in Belmont, on the peninsula south of San Francisco.

She wrote a piece about her visit to a funeral home to arrange her own burial. Her face still puffy from chemo, she read it to the hushed room:

```
Joe, the manager, showed me various combinations of
options, from the Lenin-lying-in-state model on down
to the shoebox-in-the-backyard version. I had a pleas-
ing vision of being buried in my jewelry box. When
Joe got back, I asked him if you could provide your
own container for cremated remains. He said, "Yes, but
you'd be surprised how many people neglect to bring a
lid." I said, "I guess Saran Wrap would be tacky?"
```

The laughter started when she was only halfway through, and by the time she was done the class was roaring and my dog was barking. "You *laughed*," Linda exclaimed gratefully. "I'm so glad you laughed."

In the discussion that followed, Linda's classmates suggested she drop the paragraph about driving into the funeral home parking lot and for sure keep the part where she fogged the shiny rich wood of a coffin with her breath, and asked her to make the bit about the incense clearer.

No one had the poor manners to express sympathy. Linda wasn't the dying woman here, as she was in other rooms: Here she was a writer. In this room, everything that happened, however terrible, was material. Just as the Plains Indians used every part of the buffalo, so writers, too, use everything. If it doesn't kill you, you can use it in your writing. Even—as Linda showed our class—if it does kill you.

What happens in a class? In response to assignments, you dig up stuff you'd put away as crap and find it wasn't so bad. You hear comments on another writer's piece that give you insight into a similar problem in yours (it's hard to hear direct criticism of your own babies). You hear four people say the same thing about your piece: How they didn't get how the bat swung back and cracked the catcher in the head—and you realize that you need to fiddle with that paragraph.

And you spend evenings with really smart people. At the first meeting of my classes, the writers come in and settle on my couches and chairs in the last silence that their class will know. It's like seeing people who have no idea that in six months they will be cheerfully using each other's toothbrushes. They don't know, as they dart glances at one another or stand nervously in front of the tiny marble fireplace with its sputtering Duraflame log, that they will soon arrive and leave together; that, before they know it, friendships will spring up and three of them will be renting a house on Cape Cod so they can write together during the month of August.

THE CRAFTY WRITER

Workshops you pay for are the best—it's too easy to quit when you've made no investment. I have a friend who wants to tell his story but has the misfortune to be very rich. I have no idea how to make him write. Find classes at your local bookstore, at a university extension, or online.

Join a Group

When I read book reviews that take a writer to task for lengthy digressions or embarrassing personal sections or a snippy tone, I think, *Her writing group would have pointed that out, and she'd have fixed it. If she had one.*

A writing group is a small group of writers who meet on a regular schedule, usually at one another's houses, and read or listen to one another's work. The work can be emailed ahead if it's long, or read aloud on the spot. Some groups do writing exercises together, too.

Like partners and a habitual schedule, groups pull writing out of you whether you think you're in the mood or not. Your meeting is coming up Monday night, so you scribble something during your lunch hour.

When I was working on my memoir about my teenaged daughter, *Hold Me Close*, two writer friends, Wendy Lichtman and Janis Newman, asked me to meet with them on Monday afternoons at Janis's Victorian on Liberty Street, a mile or two from my house. Janis was working on a book about adopting her son from a Russian orphanage. Wendy was writing thoughtful personal essays for magazines. I'd walk over to Janis's house with the dog, and Wendy would drive from Berkeley. The three of us would settle down with our tea and bottled water and our printouts of what we'd emailed to each other over the weekend, and begin.

I would read, and they would ask questions. How did I react to finding an empty bottle of Bacardi rum in Morgan's desk? Did I feel guilty when I read Morgan's journal? When she became pregnant and the subject of getting an abortion came up, and Morgan said, "I would never do anything like that to my baby," did I feel accused, since she knew I'd had an abortion at seventeen?

Janis would read the latest pages from her book on adopting Alex. I'd point out that here was yet another scene set in a dismal Moscow restaurant; didn't the narrator and her husband ever go anywhere else while waiting for the adoption to go through? I would exasperate Janis with my insistence on knowing exactly where everything was in relation to everything else. Wendy and I would tell her when she was being too tough on the adoption coordinator—the cat hair on the woman's skirt when she stood up, for example—did she need that mean detail? And then we'd weep over the scenes at the orphanage, when wan, sixteen-month-old Alex took his first step into his American mom's waiting arms.

Wendy would read a piece about getting her brother to stop smoking or about the series of young people who stayed with her as they were beginning their adult lives. Janis's son Alex, now a handsome gray-eyed middle schooler, would come home with his dad, and his dog, Wagner, would quietly chew up the fallen pages of my piece. The phone would ring. But on we'd talk, into the afternoon, Monday after Monday, week after week. During those months, I wasn't writing a book. I was just writing three pages for Monday.

When one of my classes ends, I now encourage the students to go on without me as a writing group, since they are on intimate terms and have a shared vocabulary for critiquing work. Here's an email from my student Bernadette Glenn about one of them:

> It's amazing how our little group has bonded. We're all writing and encouraging each other. But beyond that, there's very good work being done, being taken seriously and being published. I like it that we all look at the writing process as something vital to our lives and take it seriously, not just a hobby or for fun.

Feedback: How to Give It

You may feel at the outset that you don't have the knowledge to analyze another's piece—that you know when something doesn't sound right but don't know how to explain it or fix it. But don't worry. The knack of giving illuminating, relevant, and encouraging feedback will grow as you work on it, like any other skill.

When my first writing partner, Cynthia, and I exchanged short essays, we'd add little comments at the end of each piece. We had no idea how we were supposed to do it, having just invented our writing club, but we seemed to do all right. Her comments were specific, and often included ways to fix things. For example, in one of my pieces, I said that if I held up a sign it would say, "Will Work For Praise." Cynthia scribbled in response, "I like the point you're making here, but it doesn't work very well for me on the page. You seem to switch abruptly from specific examples of how you need praise to generalizations about people."

In a piece I wrote about how women bond by whining to each other, she remarked, "This is *so* true. But don't end with the part about your mother. Put her earlier and then say maybe she's an exception, or that maybe when you get old there's so much to complain about that there's no pointing in even starting. Come back to yourself at the very end." And in my piece about trying to improve my writing habits through hypnosis, she wrote: "This is really tied together now, and the stories are fascinating. I don't love the ending, though, even though I highlighted it. It works okay, but I'd like a little of how you felt after the experience."

BE ENCOURAGING

A successful critique is one that makes the writer want to rush to the computer to work on the piece again—not one that points out the piece's flaws in devastating detail. Keep in mind that your writing partner probably used all the courage she had just to show her work to you: She doesn't have any left to defend it from attack. Be mindful of the gulf between your response and what she is hoping to hear.

I blush to say I have not always been gentle myself. I returned a scene to my friend Janis with a comment that began, "I'm afraid this needs a lot of work." Full of myself, full of how I would write the book, I allowed myself to dwell on what wasn't working, not on what was. Janis said that when she read that first sentence she didn't dare read on, and our writing partnership ended.

So here's my advice. Don't comment on style, word choice, punctuation, and other sentence-level matters in early drafts. You're to be congratulated for recognizing a dangling modifier when you see one, but let your eye skip over it. Your partner is trying on outfits—seeing if the red blazer will work with the long black skirt and the low heels—not going out the door to the interview. Polishing comes much later, when your partner knows which sentences she'll keep, and she *is* (to keep the metaphor going) about to step out the door for the interview. Then you want to let her know she said "tenant" when she meant "tenet" (which is the orthological equivalent of having spinach in her teeth).

In the tender early stages, though, writers need to know what they're doing right, not wrong. Say things like, "This is the part that interested me" or "This is what I want to hear more of." Avoid an authoritative tone. Don't say "This isn't working for me" unless it's a toaster. Say: "This might work better if . . ." or "It might read more effectively if . . ." In other words, if you see a problem, try to suggest a solution.

Read for enjoyment, making notes only when something—too long a digression, abstract language, lack of clarity—interrupts that pleasure. The Squaw Valley Community of Writers asks workshoppers to read each piece as if it has already been accepted for publication (an approach that respects the writer's accomplishment) *before* going on to offer suggestions to improve the work.

BE SPECIFIC IN YOUR PRAISE

What especially moved you? Point out what works—in scene or dialogue or images. Be specific: "I loved your metaphors" is not as convincing as "I loved it when you compared the fat cat to a collapsed parachute."

RESPOND TO THE WRITING, NOT TO THE STORY BEING TOLD

Don't commiserate or give advice or scold or launch into your own story of being caught in a hurricane. A good way to keep the exchange "writerly," as I call it, is to refer to the protagonist of the piece as "the narrator," not as "you." Not "Why do you think that about your mother?" but "Why does the narrator think that about her mother?"

ASK QUESTIONS

Did you drift off at any point while reading? If so, tell the writer where your mind wandered, where you got bored. Where do you want him to pause, tell more? Where do you want him to speed up?

Ask "why?" frequently to help the author deepen the piece. Why would Paula believe her mother? Why was the narrator sent to her aunt? What was she hoping would happen? Why does the mother start drinking?

Is the tone working? If at any point the narrator irritates you or seems angry, let the writer know.

Does the essay have an angle? If it doesn't, help the writer kick it around.

AN EXAMPLE OF A GOOD CRITIQUE

The following is an example of an encouraging and helpful response that a writing partner gave me on an early scene in *Hold Me Close*. Her comments are in italics.

I love the stuff about your relationship with your mother, and the way it ties in here. You might want to find a slightly more graceful way to incorporate the memories of your mother. I think Morgan's statement about you getting married in high school is a good start. Maybe she can ask you what your mother thought about that?

Morgan was on the bed, crying at my new coldness. "You're so mean! You never used to talk to me this way."

"What do you expect?" I said helplessly. "After all the shit you pulled."

"You did a lot of stuff, too," she sobbed. "You got married when you were still in high school! You did whatever you wanted to!" *How does that make you feel?*

I went to sit in the kitchen. I looked at the white plate my mother had stolen from our wedding *Is this your wedding to Bill or the one in high school?* and then returned to us with pink roses and congratulations painted on it. *Nice.* I shifted my gaze, and there on the opposite wall was the black and white photograph of my mother that I'd found and blew up, her standing at the sink with a cup of coffee in her hand, wearing a man's shirt with the sleeves rolled up and a denim skirt, exactly the way she always looked.

Morgan was still crying loudly, and I remembered one day when I was sixteen. I had called her at work. *This gets confusing I thought you called Morgan; stick with your mother here.* As I waited for the busboy to get her, I could see her coming hurriedly to the phone, wiping her hands on the cloth tucked into her black belt, her notebook in one pocket of her black skirt, the other *pocket?* already sagging with the quarters (that always lined the bottom of her big black purse). *Right now the quarters are in her pock-et.* Even while picking up the phone near the dishwashing room, she'd be mentally juggling ten items, the Petrale sole ready for pickup, the table that had already asked twice for more coffee, the paper tablecloths fluttering on the tables on the grass and needing to be anchored with ashtrays. *You might know a little bit too much here. Maybe you could show us this with some overheard dialogue before she gets on the phone.*

While critiques can be enormously helpful, particularly in the early stages of a piece, be aware that the very act of critiquing can lead a writer to assume the piece needs revision of some kind. But that's not always true. Mark Childress, author of *Crazy in Alabama*, led a workshop in which the participants peppered the writer with suggestions. He listened to it all and then said, "All this story lacks is a stamp." He told the writer to send it to the *New Yorker*, which published it.

Feedback: How to Take It

Receiving a critique gracefully is another, equally important skill. As Franklin P. Jones said, "Honest criticism is hard to take, particularly from a relative, a friend, an acquaintance, or a stranger."

My student Kristin Lund summed up what a lot of writers are really thinking when someone reads a piece they've written. This is what Kristin would like to say to you, the reader:

I only wonder what you're really thinking if it is something original and pithy about my seminal work that you would like to share. For example, if you're really thinking, "This is the most poignant essay I've ever read on the agony of having a beloved ferret mistaken for a rat," think on. However, if you are really thinking, "Just kill me now. Don't make me sit here through

any more of this crap dying of ennui," feel free to
keep that to yourself. And just because you use words
like *ennui* doesn't make you any better that the rest of
us. It just makes you boring in French.

Don't we all, really, agree with Kristin? It would be great if all
critiques were along the lines of, "This is perfect! I hate you! Send
it out!" Yet the ability to hear thoughtful, constructive, honest criticism is pretty important for a writer. If you curl into a little ball
when someone questions your use of a semicolon on page three, you
will find it hard to progress. I know a talented would-be author of
children's books who responds to critiques as if he's been told he's
a worthless person. His books are not published, and that's too bad,
because he's a good writer.

Sometimes it's easier to hear a critique after you've had time to
cool off from the shock. I was in despair when I got my first letter from
my editor at Broadway Books concerning the manuscript of *Hold Me
Close*—she didn't understand me or my book at all! It took me at least a
year—by which time the book was out—for me to realize how insight-
ful she was. (I have quoted from that letter elsewhere in this book.)

It's the same thing with the irritating remarks folks closer to home
might make. "I don't know, Dare," my mother said to me when I gave
her some early pages of *The Granny Diaries*. She nodded her head doubt-
fully at the sheaf of typed papers on the coffee table. "The part about
the funny names kids give their grandmothers seems to go on too long."
I seethed, and picked up my pages huffily. Later, though, I was able to
improve the book quite a bit by editing down the part on names.

HOW DO YOU KNOW A CRITIQUE IS GOOD?

How will you know when a response to your writing is constructive and worth listening to? When the ball in the pinball machine
sinks perfectly into the slot. When you think, *Yes*. When your reader's response zeros in on something in the piece that's been nagging
at you, and you find yourself slapping your forehead and saying, "I
knew I'd have to change that part!" When the critique points out the

strengths of the writing in specific ways so you know what you're doing right, and at the same time provides suggestions for improvement. A critique is good when after you read it your fragile little seed of excitement blooms rather than withers.

CLARIFY WHAT KIND OF RESPONSE YOU WANT

Maybe you just want to know if what you said is what your reader heard. Maybe you want detailed suggestions for revision, even if it means tearing the piece up and practically starting over. Or perhaps, at an early stage, you just want them to acknowledge that you did the writing. In *Truth & Beauty*, Ann Patchett's memoir of a friendship with Lucy Grealy, she says that Lucy and her friend Joy swore never to read the pieces they dutifully sent each other. Ann explained, "In doing this we had the obligation without the judgment. Whoever failed to meet their weekly quota was committed to clean the other's bathroom."

AVOID SNARKY READERS

Does your reader say, "Is it fair to your husband to publish this?" If so, replace her. She's not paying attention to the writing. Avoid anybody who doesn't seem to get you, anybody who is distracted by grammatical errors, anybody who is not wholeheartedly on your side.

GET INPUT EARLY

Get responses *early*, before you've poured six months into the piece and will be found stocking up on lethal Tylenol if a partner timidly asks you if you really need the scene where the aunt loses her umbrella. (On the other hand, if you show a piece too early, you may not be ready to hear criticism of your still-smoking prose. I didn't say this was easy. As we'll see in the next chapter, writing is revising—a process in which a perceptive partner is invaluable.)

PROCEED WITH CAUTION: HUSBANDS, WIVES, AND MOTHERS AS READERS

My husband, Bill, was my unpaid column editor, reading first drafts and steering me away from sophomoric attempts at satire. "Not your voice," he'd say. He's in publishing, which means he had some practice in telling life and writing apart. Generally, though, mates aren't the best choice of readers. It may be hard to get the straight scoop. Your husband doesn't want to lie next to a seething creature who's just been told the short story she spent the summer working on was "fine, dear" or "all over the place."

I heard that every time Virginia Woolf finished a novel, she'd take it to her husband, Leonard, to read, and he'd say the same thing every time: "Well, you've done it again, Virginia." That's what you want to hear from your spouse.

Once you have realized what you need to improve in your piece—either from a writing partner's helpful responses or your own insights—you're ready to begin revising, a process you would be well advised to learn to love. You have no choice, if you want to get good. The desire to revise is what separates the professional writer from the journal keeper.

nine

~~REVISING~~ REWRITING YOUR WORK

**Revision is one of the true pleasures of writing.
I love the flowers of afterthought.**

—BERNARD MALAMUD

WHEN I was hired by *Departures* magazine for a 3,500-word cover story on San Francisco, I was thrilled to have the chance to write about the city I was born in. There was a catch, though: another writer had been given the assignment first and had his piece rejected, so the pressure was on.

I started in June. I interviewed people and worked on the piece all summer, even taking my notes on vacation to Tahoe and working on it amid the bottles of suntan lotion, with my husband, Bill, fidgeting in the background hinting that the trails got hot by noon. I compared San Francisco to Italian hill towns and to Rome, which also has forty-two hills. I interviewed everybody from Armistead Maupin, author of *Tales of the City*, to columnist Herb Caen. In September, I was done. I proudly gave it to Bill to read, then kind of hung around the kitchen. I scrubbed the counter and listened for little intakes of breath, little involuntary smiles.

There weren't any. He scowled, blew his breath out. He rubbed the back of his head. He knew how hard I'd worked on that piece. He knew it was due in three weeks. He knew he had to live in the same house with me. And still he turned up his hands and blurted, "Jesus, Sweetie, this is a mess. I don't even know what it's about."

That was a bad day. I saw myself calling the editor and saying, "I just can't do it, I'm sorry," and leaving him with a big hole in the magazine.

Before doing that, I tried one last thing. I called my friend Mary Roach. Now the famous author of *Stiff*, *Spook*, and *Bonk*, she then wrote funny articles about sumo wrestlers and holes in the ozone in Patagonia for national magazines such as *Vogue* and *Discovery*. Mary met me at Chevy's restaurant on Van Ness. She is skinny, a perfect ectomorph, with blonde hair, green eyes, and a long face. While she read through the sheets I handed her, I shoved a spoon around an empty margarita glass.

Then she looked up. "But this is so good!" she exclaimed. "You have all these great quotes and this great stuff about the city being like an Italian hill town."

I brightened. She and I came up with a rough outline for the piece, and when I went home and followed the outline, I turned what had been a mess into an essay I was proud of. The editor put it on the cover.

The lasting payoff, though, was that the next time I got stuck and discouraged, trying hard with a piece but getting nowhere, I'd think, *I've felt this way before and in the end I made it work*. That lesson—that a bad draft is a stage in the process, not a failure—would become part of me.

From what you see of photographers' work in a magazine, you'd think they shot brilliant image after brilliant image. I learned differently when I became managing editor at *San Francisco Focus* magazine. I'd watch a photographer spread his slides across the light table in front of the art director in his owlish black glasses—hundreds of shots, all of the mayor, or whatever. Many of them would be terrible— badly lit, the top of the man's head cut off, or taken with his eyes closed. Many would be all right but nothing special, and some would be stunning.

It's not an exaggeration to say it's the same for writing. You have to expose a lot of film to get what you want.

Professional writers revise more, not less, than less experienced ones. As Thomas Mann said, "A writer is person for whom writing is more difficult than it is for other people." Even the best writers expect to do many, many drafts before they're satisfied. S. J. Perelman said for him forty-two drafts were too many, thirty-seven too few, but thirty-nine just right. (Then he grumbled that he was giving away his trade secrets.) Maurice Sendak takes two years to finish one of his children's books, though each is no longer than a few hundred words.

You may not, ahem, enjoy revision. My friend and student Jackie Winspear told a class one night that rewrites reminded her of sewing lessons back in her English school. She'd hand in her apron, and the teacher would make her rip out all the stitches and say, "Try it again, Jackie." I don't know how her aprons turned out, but I do know that Jackie has seven books out in her Maisie Dobbs mystery series, so I guarantee you she has managed to get on better terms with the process of rewriting.

And here's the thing: Dashing off a piece that works immediately produces one kind of confidence. But *real* confidence, the kind that becomes part of you, comes from picking out those bad stitches and putting in better ones until you finish it.

But how do you know which stitches are bad?

Step Back from Your Draft

When you read over a piece you've just written, avoid the following two reactions:

1. This is wonderful. I must send it out to the world immediately!
2. This is such crap. I must destroy it.

Chances are it's neither; it most likely needs a little fiddling with before it's ready for prime time. We talked in the last chapter about how writing partners, groups, and so on can help you see what a piece needs, but there are ways you can do this yourself.

PUT IT AWAY

Writing is like a piece of pie: Let it cool before touching it with a knife. The Roman poet Horace is said to have waited eight years before deciding if a poem of his was any good. A day or two works, too.

In a hurry, and no one around but the dog? Here's a tip: Go to View if you're using Microsoft Word and read your piece on Reading Layout. The piece is laid out on the screen like a book, and glitches stand out. Even better, print it out. You can't see the whole thing on screen, and the medium is different—things you don't notice on the computer screen leap out at you. (All those repeated paragraphs, for example.)

PRETEND IT'S NOT YOURS

Take your work to a café, along with other stuff you like to read—the newspaper, a magazine—then approach your own pages almost as if they're someone else's, the way you size up that woman in a shop window before you realize you're looking at your reflection.

Highlight the wonderful bits, even half sentences and single words. Jot notes—where the holes are, scenes you don't need, whatever. I had the copy shop bind drafts of this book so that I could carry the manuscript around in my backpack. The advantages were numerous: I could work on it anywhere, problems stood out clearly in that booklike form, and it cheered me up to pretend it was already a book. You can also read your manuscripts on an electronic book reader, as if it were any other book. That's exactly what you want—that perspective.

READ YOUR WRITING ALOUD

Read your work to someone else, or ask someone to read it to you. I am always amazed—and you will be too—at how much the ear picks up that the eye doesn't. When you hear something read aloud, you don't have to search for awkward or boring parts—you'll *hear* them. Read it to the cat if no one else will listen. Did you know that blind Milton chanted *Paradise Lost* to his daughters?

You might even want to record yourself reading your work aloud. (When you play it back, you won't have to concentrate on reading—just listening.) Notice when your attention wanes—perhaps at unnecessary explanations, too many names without accompanying identification or images, too many abstract statements, too little tension. Once you've identified the parts where the piece seems to need work, you can think about rewriting them. Below are some more specific suggestions for revising.

Fix the Beginning

Your opening sentences are pretty important, considering the modern reader's attention span. Here's a cool trick: Don't bother to write the beginning in the first drafts. Just start by saying, "And another thing about (subject) . . ." You will find your beginning later; it might be something in the last paragraph or something in the middle. Once you have the good sentences, the ones with energy, move them to the top and start with them. If you love the second page because of how it sounds, capture that tone in the first sentence and keep it going for the whole piece. Hook us, at all costs.

START THE PIECE FURTHER IN

A piece about your divorce should not start with, "Once I had a bulldog named Clyde." (You can probably tell all these examples are real.) Start the piece where the trouble starts. If your piece is about not wanting to push your angry brother up a hill in his wheelchair, don't begin in the hospital where you learned the extent of his injuries. Dive in right there at the bottom of the hill, where your loathed brother is smoking a forbidden cigar and cursing you for your weak arms. Flash back to the past only as needed to fill us in.

I really do mean "as needed." We need a lot less backstory than you might think. An injured person became injured at some point, a person finishing a hike started out somewhere, a car on the side of the road was once on the road, a woman getting a divorce once met her husband and married him. We are modern moviegoing readers: we understand the quick cut.

My student Melody Cryns said of her own tendency for the leisurely beginning:

> In the piece about my daughter Megan and her cheerleading squad not making it to Regionals, I started at the beginning—before the competition. Well, actually, I started with watching the Canada geese fly in formation, which made me think of how the girls on the cheerleading squad all stand in formation, which made me think of . . . anyway. Now I jump in right when the action starts.

If you start too far back, you risk boring your readers with background information they don't yet care about and thus won't remember anyway. You'll be forced to summarize, skip over stuff, and generalize. Anton Chekhov knew this. His advice? "Tear your story in half and start in the middle." After the exciting lead you can take us back to the beginning, if you need to, because we're hooked.

My student Lucas Peltonen begins right in the middle of things in an essay called "The Hospitalization":

> The hospital orderly left me sitting in the wheelchair in the middle of the hallway in direct line of the blowing wind and snow. He trudged down the hall to the wide-open double doors that were allowing New York City's biggest snowstorm in fifty years to blow into the hallway. Tufts of snow were already forming along the walls. I was wearing nothing more than my underwear and a thin hospital gown with a gap running up the back.

Once we are sufficiently worried about the man left in the teeth of a gale, the author can go back to the beginning of the trouble: "I attended a personal training seminar all day, but I knew from the moment I woke up that morning that I was in trouble."

SURPRISE US

You can also start with an astonishing statement that hooks the reader, as my students do in these examples:

```
The first time I saw my son, Alex, he was eleven months
old. (Janis Cooke Newman)

I just hung up the phone with my mother (in her six-
ties), who was visiting my mother-in-law (in her eight-
ies). They were getting stoned. (Mary Patrick)

You want to know how to meet a man? I'll tell you how
to meet a man. Put an ad in your local paper for a 1977
Chevy Malibu Classic. (Penny Wallace)
```

Fix the Ending

Endings can be one of the hardest parts of a first-person piece. Sit back, look over the piece, and ask yourself two questions:

1. What, really, is going on here?
2. How do I feel about it?

EXPERIMENT WITH ORDER

Your real ending, like your real beginning, may be buried elsewhere in the piece—move things around and see. As an experiment, print out the pages and cut them apart with a pair of scissors, moving paragraphs around to see whether a different order would be more interesting.

MAKE SURE THERE *IS* AN ENDING

Of course moving paragraphs around won't work if your piece has no ending, as can happen when you write from life. If your subject is buying a house and cactus garden near remote Mono Lake, California, for example, and you are still torn over whether moving there from East 57th Street in Manhattan was a good idea, you can't yet write an essay with a conclusion. Unresolved, ongoing stories—your conflict with your sister, your penchant for picking the wrong men, your patients with their same old yarns—sometimes don't work because you are still mired in the problem. You have to wait until you can tell us what happened at the end.

If you're not sure whether you have an ending or not, summarize your story in 200 words or less. Here's an example from a student exercise:

> My father was going to die. I knew that if I didn't confront him with all these angry feelings I had that I would be stuck with them after he died. I confronted him at his house in Portland, Oregon, and told him how angry I was at him, and threw a camera on the floor. He was amazed. Not mad—amazed that I felt that way. He had no idea. I felt much freer after that. And then he didn't die. So we had around ten years after that in which we had a nice relationship with most of the baggage just dropped overboard.

As we saw back in chapter 3, the end of a personal essay often contains the epiphany (what the narrator realized) and the resolution (what the narrator did next as a result). A humor piece, in contrast, can end with a snappy line.

BRING BACK AN IMAGE

Here's a neat technique you can try on one of your shorter essays: Look back at your first paragraph and grab an image or idea from it to repeat at the end. This will give the reader the comforting feeling of having come full circle. A travel editor once complimented me on how in the first paragraph of my piece I had my boyfriend tying my kids' little red sleeping bags to the top of his Volvo, and in the final paragraph I had the sleeping bags falling off the car. I hadn't even noticed the sleeping bag thing, but of course I didn't tell the editor that. (Later I discovered it's called a *tie-back ending*.)

try this

Write out the plot of five of your pieces. Ask yourself these questions: What's the problem? Why does it matter? What backstory do we need? What actions are taken? What are the obstacles (inner and outer)? Is there a resolution?

Fix in General

Of course half of the chapters in this book can be regarded as suggestions for revising your work. The following are a few specific issues and strategies to think about as you tackle a second draft.

KNOW WHEN TO CUT

This is what Carolyn Chute told the magazine *Writers Ask*:

```
I write a lot of junk. On and on and on, all this junk.
But every now and then this dramatic moment happens,
so I lift that out and put that aside. And then I write
all this junk: they're brushing their teeth, they're
sitting there, they're looking around—you know. Then
something will happen and I'll pull that out. Because
those are the only strong things.
```

Do what Carolyn Chute does. Cross out what's boring. You can't fix boring. Cross out the junk, keep what's good. Take out the dull anecdote about the aunt and put in a better one about the uncle who

liked to knit. Cut anecdotes, paragraphs, and images that don't move
the story forward or that repeat something we already know or that
threaten to take us off the topic. If the piece is about what it feels like
to be at a ballgame, how did those two paragraphs deploring players'
huge salaries sneak in there?

Don't be afraid to cut, even when doing so leaves you with a big
hole in your piece. You'll find something better to fill it, though you
may have to let some time go by before the right lines come to you.

Samuel Johnson advised, "When reading something you have
written, if you come across a passage that seems to you extraordinarily
fine, cut it out." This is popularly called murdering your darlings. That
section on the trip to Paris—it's lyrical and fine, isn't it? Sure, it may
be somewhat of a deviation, but everybody *loves* the Paris section.
What you said about the shuttered book kiosks, the streets filled with
rain, the . . . never mind. It has to go. The reader doesn't need to hear
about Paris to understand why your marriage blew up. Any sentence,
paragraph, scene, or chapter, no matter how powerful, that serves no
story purpose is just so many wasted words.

THE CRAFTY WRITER

You don't have to part from your cherished (yet unnecessary) passages
forever. Try moving that darling down to the bottom of the page under "Notes." That way it's nearby, where you can visit it anytime you
want to remind yourself what a fabulous writer you are. One friend of
mine makes a separate file, entitled "Scraps," and dumps the deleted
material there, promising herself she can always go back to it if she
wants. She's never wanted to yet.

SAVE EVERYTHING

Just because the bit about the bear doesn't work in this story doesn't
mean it won't be the perfect anecdote to use in another one. Don't
throw out anything! Change the file name with each revision so you
don't wipe out the old version. Your best writing is mixed up with

your worst. If you throw out the worst, you risk throwing out the best. All your writing, whether it's outtakes from stories or abandoned drafts, becomes part of your inventory. Your inventory is the sketches, notes, half-finished pieces, and finished pieces that will be your material, your trunk of fabric remnants.

FILL IN THE HOLES

Adding is just as important as cutting. Let's start with adding *context*. It's surprising how many writers will neglect to tell us where we are, when it is, and who is talking to us, thus plunging us into a tale that takes place nowhere in particular, at no time in particular, and happens to no one in particular. We get streets without names, houses missing their neighborhoods, towns floating on the map, conversations that happen in limbo.

You can give us this needed context in a sentence or two. Instead of having an unknown narrator pop up talking about whatever is on her mind, give us a quick who-when-where: "We were in Venice, my friend Joan and I, girlfriends on a mission to find culture and wine among the alleys and canals of the old city."

A narrator can introduce herself, instead of assuming that the reader knows as much as she does about where and who she is. In this example, the narrator situates herself in a vivid setting, tells us what she's doing, and provides a clue about her age: "I sat in the backseat of our green Dodge Dart waiting for my mom. We were parked outside the house of our friends, the Zasloffs, on a street lined with towering oaks." Don't be reluctant to give us the simple facts: "James was Jane's older brother." We won't think less of you for writing what you may consider a boring sentence. We will feel comforted and grateful to know who James is, and will be able to concentrate on what you're about to tell us.

Here's another example of some nicely informative sentences, written by my student Shannon Falk: "When I was eight months pregnant with our first child, my husband was diagnosed with metastatic stage four cancer. If the disease was rated in the same way as hurricanes it would be a Category 5."

try this

If your story is about a loss, let us see what things were like *before* it happened. For instance, if you've written about your father's death, show him alive—preferably in a scene with you.

- Rewrite a piece from memory, without looking at it, to see what new ideas come up.

- Expand important paragraphs (ones that contain turning points) from pieces you've written, adding images, details, and the narrator's emotional response to what is happening.

- Add three sentences after every existing sentence you've already written, to see what else is there. This is, truly, a terrific exercise. I have my students do this, especially those who race through a complex story in three pages. For example, let's say you wrote, "I woke up. I got dressed." You'd have to add three more sentences in between those lines: "I woke up. *Something had pulled me out of the dream about a giant squid wearing sunglasses. I listened, but heard only the backfire of a car passing on the street. My muddy pants and shirt lay in a heap on the rug next to the bed.* I got dressed."

INCLUDE TIME AND DISTANCE

Chronology holds a story together. People must know the *when* of it. Let us know how events are related in time: "the next Saturday" or "two months later." (If you're writing something lengthy, you might even want to write out a timeline.) You don't have to know exactly when something happened. Occasionally you can say, "sometime later . . ." But even "sometime later" gives a nod to our need for chronology. The same idea applies to distance—we need to have a sense of how far apart important places are. So if you're going to your mother's house, tell us where she lives, where you live, and the distance between.

SPEED UP, SLOW DOWN: ADJUST YOUR PACE

Speed us through the less important parts of your story with a single image or two: "For the next two weeks, we crossed the country, discarded McDonald's wrappers eddying behind our seats." Slow down when things get interesting, when you want to reader to notice something or feel something. This is called *pace*. My friend Donna Levin, author of *California Street*, read a draft of my memoir and said, "Choose the most compelling points and stay with them. For example, picking Morgan up at the police station. Instead of the paragraph or two you give it, re-create it. Put in seeing other people there to bail out loved ones."

Pace applies not only to events but to characters as well. The more important a person is in your story, the more you should describe him or her. The cashier who hands you your receipt can be a blur, but when you open the door to see your supposedly dead husband grinning on the doorstep, donning the Stanford sweatshirt he wore on the cruise ship he supposedly fell off, slow down.

KNOW WHEN TO ABANDON A PIECE

Sometimes it's worth admitting that something just isn't working. It might be that the piece turns out to be the scaffolding—not worth keeping itself, but what you needed to get somewhere else. (For instance, you may be writing about realizing that you'd left Salt Lake City for Sacramento to escape a boyfriend, but then it dawns on you that the reader doesn't care why you left Salt Lake City. The reader wants to hear about moving to a strange city alone at the age of twenty. You're focused on the boyfriend, but we're thinking, *Boy, I could never do that, just plunk myself down in a strange city without knowing anybody. How did you do that? How did it feel?*)

Sometimes a piece lacks essential elements, or the tone is wrong and can't be fixed, or it simply isn't surprising enough. Believe me when I say an entire project that you've been creating for years can be one big darling that needs murdering. It's painful to turn your back on something you've poured your heart and your time into. But even a forest needs the occasional fire for seeds to sprout. If you toss a moribund project, you might produce a creative vacuum into which a waiting work will rush. It's like breaking up with a bad boyfriend before you can meet a good one.

Fix the Sentences

When your piece or book is roughly ready—the beginning works, the tone is right, you've adjusted the pace, you like the ending—you may allow yourself the pleasure of fiddling with the sentences. What follows here is a list (in no particular order) of suggestions for ways to do that.

GET A GRIP ON GRAMMAR

I assume that you have grammar and punctuation under control. If you don't, for Pete's sake have somebody look over your pieces before you send them out, or you'll look like an idiot. If your writing is peppered with errors, the person you're trying to impress will be thinking more about the holes in your education than about what you're saying. And beware of relying on spell-check—it can't tell the difference between scared and scarred, roles and rolls, bear and bare.

Okay, one quick section on punctuation. In American English, the quotation mark goes *outside* the period and the comma.

>   YES: "The furnace has two functions," I said. "Dysfunc-
>   tional and sauna."
>   NO: "The furnace has two functions", I said. "Dysfunc-
>   tional and sauna".

Use two hyphens to indicate a dash--like that. Don't capitalize the names of the seasons. And don't capitalize directions (north, south, east, west) unless they mean regions.

>   YES: That summer, I went east until I arrived at the
>   East Coast.

```
NO: That Summer, I went East until I arrived at the
east coast.
```

When quoting interior thoughts, use italics, not quotation marks.

```
YES: Who doesn't know that? I thought.
NO: "Who doesn't know that?" I thought.
```

Also, go easy on interior monologue. Editors view it as a sign of weak writing, and large amounts of italics are not easy to read. While you're at it, limit rhetorical questions, too (*Why had I come here? What was I expecting to find?*).

IDENTIFY PEOPLE ON FIRST MENTION

Don't assume the reader knows who "we" is. The reader doesn't live with you. Consider the following sentence:

```
The door to the parlor was always locked. We went in
there only around Christmas.
```

Who is "we"? We can guess it's you and your siblings, but that's what we're doing—guessing. Save your readers the frustration of guessing and provide some clarity:

```
The door to the parlor was always locked. My twin
brother, Oliver, and I went in there only around
Christmas.
```

SHOW WHERE PEOPLE ARE

The following sentence doesn't anchor readers in a specific location, which makes it difficult to imagine the scene:

```
When I returned the volume to my father, I said to him,
"Teach me architecture."
```

Where is the narrator? Where is his father? Instead write:

```
When I went into the sparsely furnished study to re-
turn the volume to my father, I said to him, "Teach me
architecture."
```

PICK A TENSE—PAST OR PRESENT

Choosing the right tense can be perplexing in autobiographical writing, which can shift from past to present so much. Present tense adds immediacy, past tense a sense of depth.

```
PAST: The dog rushed out. I caught him by the collar.
PRESENT: The dog rushes out. I catch him by the collar.
```

The past tense is best for most purposes. But it's up to you which tense to employ. Just make it consistent.

OMIT THE OBSERVING FILTER AND "BEGAN TO . . ."

In any first-person narrative, it's obvious that what's being noticed is being noticed by the narrator, so cut phrases like "I noticed," "I observed," and so on.

```
YES: He wore two vests, one on top of the other.
NO: I noticed that he wore two vests, one on top of the
other.
```

Also, avoid having your characters *start* or *begin* to do something, unless the rhythm of the sentence demands it.

```
YES: He writes.
NO: He starts to write.

YES: I threw up.
NO: I began to throw up.
```

See how much tighter the first options are?

BEWARE OF ADVERBS AND ADJECTIVES

My student Metece Ricco loved adverbs and adjectives. She wrote:

> Never one to pass up a **shining** opportunity for worry,
> I was **busily** fretting over the mountain of **unfinished**
> paperwork that loomed **accusingly** on my desk. I had just
> begun brooding over whether I'd gotten overcharged by
> that plumber who had **hastily** fixed my leaky toilet last
> Saturday, when it hit me: I felt good. After thirteen
> months of feeling **perpetually** exhausted, as if some
> **efficient** vampire was **systemically** draining my life
> blood, I **actually** felt healthy again.

Look at the passage. What does *busily* add to *fretting*? Isn't all paperwork unfinished? Isn't all *looming* accusing? All vampires can be assumed to be efficient unless an inept one comes along to say otherwise. The one adverb I would keep, or at least keep the meaning it conveys, is *hastily*, as it's important to show the plumber did the job suspiciously fast.

When I said all this to Metece, she laughed. "I still cling protectively to my adverbs," she said later in a letter, and enclosed a batch of red Christmas balls to hang from my tree, each with an adverb written in gold leaf. One of them, of course, said *protectively*.

AVOID FLABBY VERBS

Often you reach for an adverb when the real problem in the sentence is a flabby verb—with the chief culprit being the verb *to be*. Why use that weak little auxiliary verb to say, "He was skiing down the hill" when you can say, "He skied down the hill"? "There was a man standing on the corner" can be "A man stood on the corner." That last sentence brings up another point: the phrases "There is" and "There was" can usually be replaced with a more active verb. For instance, "There was a fire" can be "A fire broke out."

Scan your prose for slacker verbs. Instead of, "We were on Highway 101, going like quicksilver," you could write, "A quicksilver drive sucked us down Highway 101." Also try to use interesting verbs, such as "pebbled under the skin" as opposed to "collected under the skin."

OTHER MUSHY ADVERBS, ADJECTIVES, AND PHRASES TO AVOID

Whenever possible, steer clear of the following words and phrases: *almost, appears, eventually, practically, basically, finally, somehow, sort of, really, usually, awfully, quite, ultimately, utterly, kind of, actually, definitely,* and *very.*

Never use the word *literally* at all. You will mean *figuratively,* as did the cookbook author who said she literally cooked recipes in her head. Or if you do mean literally, people won't get the distinction you're making because everybody uses this word wrong. I just read a newspaper piece that quoted a broker saying, "People have literally picked up their house at the foundation and shook it upside down like a piggy bank." I have another in front of me, from *Apartment Magazine,* which says, "You can literally see the lightbulb come on over people's heads." Don't such bloopers figuratively make you see red?

NITPICKING PRESENT PARTICIPLES

In this case, we're not replacing an incorrect usage with a correct one. We're just talking about getting rid of all that "ing" word flab that plagues sentences. Notice the difference between the original sentences and the rewritten ones:

> ORIGINAL: "The airport's over there," he said, pointing out the window.
> REWRITE: He pointed out the window. "The airport's over there."
>
> ORIGINAL: "Well, that's that!" she said, putting the car in gear and pulling out onto the street.
> REWRITE: She put the car in gear. "Well, that's that!" she said. She pulled out onto the street.

The original constructions aren't wrong, but the pros rarely use them.

BEWARE OF BODY PARTS ACTING ON THEIR OWN

Hands, fingers, and other body parts don't do things. *You* do things.

```
ORIGINAL: My eyes looked away.
REWRITE: I looked away.
```

```
ORIGINAL: My hands fiddled with the clasp of my purse.
REWRITE: I fiddled with the clasp of my purse.
```

WORK LIKE A DOG TO GET RID OF CLICHÉS

Overused phrases don't evoke a strong reaction in the reader. Do any of the following sentences strike you as vivid or memorable? *Chills ran up and down my spine. The mother of all writing courses. A heartbeat away from the presidency. A perfect storm.*

We all sink into a chair when we hear bad news, and feel the hair standing up on the backs of our necks when we're scared. So how do you describe a familiar feeling in a new way? That's the challenge of writing. You may have to write down ten familiar images until you hit on something new.

I would also steer clear of familiar phrases like "Trust me," "let's face it," and "Don't get me wrong."

How Do You Know When You're Finished?

Once you've revised the piece and polished the sentences, you're done. You know you're finished when you catch yourself changing stuff and then putting it back to the way you had it before. Or when the piece gets worse, not better, the more you fiddle with it. Or when you can't find anything in the piece to fix.

If any of those are the case, you're finished. Back away. You don't want to be one of those people who begin dusting in the basement and are found in the attic twelve hours later polishing jam jars. (Or like the painter Pierre Bonnard, who would sneak into museums and rework his canvases. I also heard of a sculptor who followed his statue as it was wheeled into the museum in a cart, and carved it as he ran alongside.)

PART IV

THE

MEMOIR

ten

PLANNING YOUR MEMOIR

Writing has laws of perspective, of light and shade just as painting does, or music. If you are born knowing them, fine. If not, learn them. Then rearrange the rules to suit yourself.

—TRUMAN CAPOTE

Forgive me if I'm being overly obvious, but a memoir is, of course, a book. That means it's at least 50,000 words long. A memoir (not pronounced mem-wah, please!) is the book-length story of how you desperately wanted something, how you went about getting it, and what you found out about yourself along the way. It's about one particular event, relationship, or theme, and usually covers a shorter time period than do memoirs, with an *s*, which are more loosely organized collections of stories and anecdotes going back through the author's entire life. (Those tend to be written by celebrities, and devoured at poolside). In his memoir, *It's Not About the Bike*, for example, Lance Armstrong wrote about his battle with cancer, not about his whole life. A biography, in contrast to either a memoir or memoirs, is the complete story of a life. You don't get one of those unless you are famous.

Will Your Idea Work?

You may already have something in mind to write about. You were shot by your husband's lover. You started your own outlaw radio station. You renounced the life of a wealthy socialite to become a nun. A carelessly parked van careened downhill and plucked the husband from your side, or you tried to kill yourself after a disastrous love affair. Is your idea going to pan out, be worth the sacrifices and the learning curve it will take to write it? A memoir means at least a year of typing and retyping and printing out and eating Cheerios out of the box and skipping parties. Writing one is enormously satisfying. But it's harder than it looks, so it makes sense to start by making sure your idea will work.

FIRST, IS IT OVER?

If you're still getting chemo or arguing with your ex-spouse over who gets the golden retriever or sporting the shaved head of your cult, you may not be ready to put the experience into perspective. Certainly it's going to be hard to come up with an ending.

This was one of the mistakes I made. I wrote my own memoir, *Hold Me Close, Let Me Go,* for a reason many people do: Something hard happened in my life. At thirteen, my daughter Morgan was the cyclone. I was the trailer park. She sneaked out of the house at night, smoked, drank, lied. As she got older, things got much, much worse. In a scene at the beginning of my book, in fact, I am watching my pregnant teenage daughter pack. She is not running away: I am throwing her out of the house.

When I made notes for a book about those years, I had no idea that writing a memoir was anything more than just writing down what happened. *Type, type, type.* I was already writing a 700-word column about my life twice a week—wasn't a memoir just, well, longer?

Oh, boy. The mistakes. It was as if I decided to build a house and just started nailing together boards without even thinking about a blueprint. I wrote the first draft when my little hell-child was still a dyed-head, baggy-jeaned seventeen. There I was, tapping away at my

Dell in one room while she was on the phone in another, arranging to meet her druggie boyfriend. I hadn't even gotten my sense of humor back. When I complained to Morgan's dad, Jim, that when she forgot her keys she tore a hole in the fence and broke into my house, he said, "But look how badly she wanted to come home." Only years later did I recognize the humor in it.

A friend looked at the first draft for me and said it reads like "a report from the trenches." She added cautiously, "Are you sure you're ready to write this?"

I let more time—years, in fact—go by, and tried again. That same friend read the new pages, and, now not bothering to conceal her dismay at the first draft, wrote:

> The draft you sent me last round concentrated on the mess of life with Morgan and I felt mired in it. This one is more reflective and concentrates primarily on you and your process, which I find more interesting. It still reflects all your feelings of deep confusion and betrayal, but because you seem to have developed more detachment, I can follow the events as part of a story rather than as an ongoing assault.

D'Arcy Fallon, author of a memoir about the period she spent as a young woman on a Marin County commune, said in her note to the reader:

> I needed a lot of distance to write So Late, So Soon. It percolated inside me for nearly three decades before I could love the person I had once been and begin to see my brethren with appreciation, humor, and compassion. By the time I started writing, I wasn't angry but oddly . . . curious about us all, as if my life at the Lighthouse Ranch had happened to someone else.

Even if you're not ready to write actual pages, *do take notes*! They will be invaluable later on. It's like taking a home video: That boring footage of everyone chatting at the table? It will be riveting in ten years. I began taking notes when Morgan was thirteen. Here's a sample entry that was useful when it came time to write the memoir:

```
Saw the actual report card yesterday. 4 Ws. Morgan had
friends over, new clothes from The Gap, dark red lip-
stick on, and I was so mad I could hardly be in the same
room with her. They bought hugely oversized jeans and
shirts, like clown clothing. She did her homework with
a pink marker, three or four words to each piece of
binder paper. At around 3 a boy came over, with a name
something like Balloon, and they drifted out together.
```

Write the notes in images, in literary style, not in journalese. "Felt terrible again this Thursday" won't do much good when you sit down to write the essay or the book. You think at the time it's fascinating when you're recording your feelings, but later you'll wish you'd jotted down exactly what people said, what happened, and how the sedan got that flat tire in the first place.

Caveat: Don't let the journal dictate the book when it comes time to write it. Journals are daily jottings in which whatever is set down is important at the time, but may not be in the bigger picture. You might end up with ten scenes that show you getting fed up with your fiancé, because it kept happening, but we only need to see it once in the book. A journal might show you just reacting to the next bad thing that happens, whereas in a book we want to see you taking steps to resolve your problems. Regard your journal as a set of notes to which you refer for details—not as the blueprint for your story.

SECOND, ARE YOU A VICTIM OR A HERO?

Let's assume that the experience you want to write about has been over long enough for you to have some perspective on it. Now you need to ask yourself whether you're a victim or a hero in your story.

If you are a victim, the book will not work. Being a victim includes illness, the perfidy of husbands, the shock of being fired, betrayed, cheated, having imperfect parents, and so on. Remember what I said in chapter 3 about (excuse me again) Shit Happens?

A good memoir is not about the painful blow that life unfairly dealt you. It's about what happened next. It's about how human beings change under pressure, not about the bad things that can happen to people. That we can get from the evening news.

If you marry a doctor who turns out to be a crook, that's not change. It's bad luck. If you marry a doctor who turns out to be a crook, and you knew all along something was wrong—those unexplained phone calls, a repossessed Porsche—then you have a story to tell. It will be about what you found out about yourself, not about him, the night of his arrest.

Like an essay, a memoir should show how the tale changed the teller. How someone pinned down by life finds a way to move forward. How someone comes to terms with grief. A father who had refused to see the evil in his son realizes his own poor judgment. A resentful employee finally sees that she, not her jerk of a boss, is the one keeping her trapped in her job—and quits. A cult member recognizes that his group *is* a cult—and leaves. My writing partner Janis Newman wanted to become a mother, and adopted a Russian boy. She ends her memoir, *The Russian Word for Snow*, with this:

> I looked back into his eyes, and at that moment I knew that I would forever put myself between him and all the dangers of the world—a vicious dog, a speeding car, a bullet from a gun. I had become a mother.

In my case, I learned that when I was feeling most like a failure—grounding Morgan only to watch her go out a window, taking her to drug counseling only to have her quit—I was doing my job as a mother, because she saw how hard I was trying, and that was a strong message in itself. My message to the reader was, sure, you might do the wrong thing. But keep trying.

THIRD, WILL PEOPLE WANT TO READ IT?

As I meet with more and more writers of memoir, using my Insta-Hot to make them tea and then sitting down to talk their book through, I find myself telling them a lot that *what you want to write is not always what the readers want to read*. That's a tough thing to say: "You lived through it, you can't forget it, and no one wants to hear it." Ack!

I know. But be brave, before you invest the time. Ask yourself, "Why would someone want to read this book? Why would *I* want to read it?" Don't confuse an obsession (with a boyfriend, say, or a disappointing mother) with a compelling subject. It can be an elaborate form of brooding.

Writing is something people like to think comes straight from the heart. No one says it is not enough to be honest and vulnerable, and write beautiful flowing sentences. No one says you must tell us a story. No one explains that the story of your life, of how you came to be you, needs to follow guidelines and have a hero, a quest, obstacles overcome, lessons learned, people changed.

You want to stand back from your story with your arms folded. In a good memoir, you are like the main character in a movie. You not only have a problem but you try a lot of different things to solve your problem, have setbacks, make mistakes, learn from them, and push on. The memoir writers I've worked with include a man who was dumped by his wife and went on a diet that transformed his life; a woman who solved both her financial and relationship problems by becoming an over-forty call girl; a woman who fled the state with her child to escape his abusive father; a man who reacted to greed and excess in real estate development by virtually inventing green building in America. Those are stories with action—stories in which the narrator's own efforts affect the outcome. These stories have satisfying endings.

Not all real stories have satisfying endings. For example, one student was working on a memoir about a love affair she had with a married man when she was very young. Her appealing story of a naïve young secretary dazzled by her married boss works well until she becomes a home wrecker, seeing him in secret. And then the man

dies when the author is twenty-six, which is what happens in life—
sometimes things just stop, rather than end.

When your story is compelling but lacks a good ending, you might
want to consider fiction. Seriously—that's the answer when real life
doesn't deliver the necessary literary elements. I've been thinking
about writing about the two years my mother spent in home hospice
before she died, and all the family drama of that period, but an ailing
parent is not an action plot: I had no control over events, and thus
could only react to them. If I write about it, I may have to do it as
fiction.

Use Reflective Voice

The reader assumes you are telling your story because you now have
some insight into it: insight into why you and others behaved as you
did, into why things happened as they did. As memoirist Patricia
Hampl said, "Consciousness, not experience, is the galvanizing core
of a personal story." This means that in a memoir the author both tells
the story and interprets it. This is called *reflective voice* in a memoir and
perspective in an essay. It's the voice that comments.

In *A Slant of Sun*, Beth Kephart uses reflective voice to describe
how she feels about having an autistic son:

> It seems to me that my inability to enter my son's
> world is a personal failure, a crisis. I do not men-
> tion it to the few friends who call. I hide it from my
> family, and I decline to talk about such things with my
> husband, who somehow always understands where Jeremy's
> (toy) cars are going and why; knows, just by observ-
> ing, which car is the odd car out and free for moving.
> I can't talk to my husband because he is the better
> parent, and so in the dark at night, I lie awake and
> wonder, worry about the instincts I am lacking, and
> conclude—horrified—that love alone may not be enough.

"I lie awake and wonder, worry about the instincts I am lacking, and conclude—horrified—that love alone may not be enough." That's reflective voice: It is the voice in the book that makes sense of things. The reflective voice employs phrases such as these:

```
If this hadn't happened, I would never have . . .
It's the first time I really . . .
Before then I had felt . . .
Later I imagined . . .
Then I thought . . .
Now I realize . . .
```

In a memoir, you are two people. First, you are the harried, clueless, sweaty person living through the events as they unfold on the page, with no perspective, no idea of what's going to happen, and perhaps no idea why you behave as you do. For example, the *you then* in the story may think of her son as just a little eccentric. But there's also *you now*, the author looking back, who knows you were missing the signs of autism. Reflective voice tells us why you think you missed those signs: "I didn't want it to be true, so I told myself lots of kids sing jingles from commercials."

The reflective voice is, by the way, how you can get an adult voice in a book about your childhood. If you use the voice of the adult narrator looking back, you can get both the immediacy of the kid's view and the adult perspective. *To Kill a Mockingbird*, for example, has an adult narrator looking back. (It's a novel, I know, but an autobiographical one.) The difference can be as simple as whether you use a kid voice ("Mommy always sang as she worked") or an adult voice ("My mother always sang as she worked").

Readers grow tetchy when the author fails to offer insight into why people behaved as they did. "You're telling me this because?" we want to ask. My Limerick friend Connor wrote a memoir about his drunken Irish childhood. His vivid scenes of working on a fishing trawler and on high-rise construction jobs brought out an interesting theme: the forgiving world of fellow men, where the worst family bungling can be washed away with a pint. As I read his pages, I understood what had happened; knew what choices he'd made. But I didn't understand *why* he'd made them. Why fishing? What in him seized on this particular fantasy? Why did he decide at one point to go to Australia? On his first day of school at five years old, he went up a tree rather than into the classroom like the other boys. I wanted to know why. What is this contrary act an early indication of?

The young protagonist in Connor's story is drunk and numb much of the time. But the author is the experienced, wised-up Connor, recalling these adventures from his brownstone house in Brooklyn, telling us about his younger self's antics because he has some insight into them. He realizes now that he was trying to escape not his circumstances, but himself.

Vivian Gornick in *The Situation and the Story* says, "Good writing has two characteristics. It's alive on the page and the reader is persuaded that the writer is on a voyage of discovery." She says that J. R. Ackerley in *My Father and Myself* "is a wholly engaging man, not because he sets out to be fashionably honest but because the reader feels him actively working to strip down the anxiety till he can get to something hard and true beneath the smooth surface of sentimental self-regard."

Gornick believes that every memoir is about a flash of insight—hers was that she could not leave her mother because she had become her mother. This insight organizes the writing. She says that successful memoirists may not know any more than the rest of us, but they know who they are at the moment of writing.

John Beckman, an editor in Sonoma County, California, that I paid to read the manuscript of *Hold Me Close*, described an early draft like this:

```
Jagged, composed of too many jump cuts, rather than a
memoir that flowed and grew in understanding over time.
In a way, too much show, and not enough tell. If we had
more of your thoughts on your work, Bill, family, the
nature of the times, and how all of that fits emotion-
```

ally into the crisis, there would be more perspective. We need to make you more sympathetic to the reader, and the best way for you to do this is to step back from the narrative and comment on why you did what you did.

Grateful for such criticism, in later drafts I tried to get better at reflective voice. Trying, for example, to account for why I kept my new husband around when the tension between him and Morgan drove her into the streets, I said:

I wanted to be a good mom, wanted it desperately, even, but their childhood coincided with the prime of my life, my career, my romances, all the pleasures and distractions of an urban life. I was their mom, and this was their childhood. But at the same time, I was a woman who had just found the man she wanted to spend the rest of her life with. I was mid-span in my own life, and this was it: my chance at lasting love.

Editors and reviewers take memoirists to task for the absence of reflective voice more than for anything else. In the *New York Times*, Elsa Dixler, reviewing *Expecting to Fly* by Martha Tod Dudman, said:

Her focus on the details leaves the big questions unanswered. Why did Martha stop taking drugs? Why was she so angry at her kind, supportive parents? Was her rebellion sparked by the atmosphere of the 60s, or was it more personal? Was it safer to take those chances in the 60s than it is now? And how, really, does she feel about her experience?

MAKE CONNECTIONS

Connect events for us. Account for what people did. As E. M. Forster famously pointed out, there's a difference between saying, "The king died, and then the queen died," and "The king died, and the queen died of grief." If you don't know the answers, you can offer a guess. One student speculated on why her mother behaved as she did this way:

> Now I realize my mother's fears were so profound, and so deep, driven into her bones from the days she fled Russian revolutionaries in her mother's arms at age two, from Poland. Her first years must have been spent in terror.

The best way to incorporate reflective voice is to keep asking yourself questions and try to answer them: Why did your parents leave Oklahoma? What need, desire, or blindness made you believe your fiancé's promises? Why on earth did you sign that piece of paper—in which your spouse took title of what had been jointly owned properties—without looking at it? Why did you marry him when you had caught him in so many lies?

Why did your mother want you to be Chinese, while your father wanted you to be Chinese-American? Why did your mother take a job as a carhop? Why did your grandfather run off? Why did your parents not notice all the food you stole from the fridge in the worst stages of your bulimia? Why did you think you could sleep with someone you cared about and not get attached?

In making these connections for us, of course, you make those connections for yourself. Every time you change the writing, the writing changes you.

As we saw in the essay, questions can actually drive the book, so that the search for answers becomes part of the suspense. Debra Gwartney, author of *Live Through This: A Mother's Memoir of Runaway Daughters and Reclaimed Love*, said in *Poets & Writers* that the question of her book was not, "Why did my daughters leave me?" It was this: "Who is the woman whose daughters would leave her?"

The events of the story shed light on the question that is troubling you. Barb Cressman, who is seventy-two, is writing her life story. She says that as she's worked on her book, she's realized the two central questions she wants it to answer: "Who was I? What did I want?"

Sometimes that's all a personal narrative is—the writer replaying the events of a story while comparing those events at every point to the questions that trouble her: Am I a good person? Why do I keep picking the wrong men? Why did I make the choices I did?

Use reflective voice to account for your own actions. It's not enough to tell us that you did one hundred jigsaw puzzles in a row after your sister died. We want you to know why you did. Lynn Freed said in *Reading, Writing, and Leaving Home,* that the writer has to de-fictionalize her life, "to disentangle it from the myths and fictions that we all create in order to control what we cannot alter. And then to work down, down, down, to the morally anaerobic heart of the matter within." My student Erika Johnson reflected on why she got married so fast:

> Even at thirty-three, I was old enough to have experienced the consequences of sliding into romantic relationships for no real reason except that the opportunity presented itself, and specifically the opportunity to care for another person. As finicky, even obsessive, as I could be in terms of my environment—the structured way in which I went about my life—I knew I was surprisingly sloppy in the manner in which I made decisions.

AVOID MENTIONING SHRINKS

Of course the insights in a memoir can echo the realizations of psychotherapy, so it's useful to remember Chekhov's advice: "Shun all descriptions of the characters' spiritual state. You must try to have that state emerge from their actions." Imagine Flaubert writing about the childhood trauma that made Madame Bovary unfaithful to her husband, or Anna Karenina, not hit by the train after all, sniffling into tissues as she pours her heart out at tedious length to her shrink. Or Romeo and Juliet discussing their relationship with a couples counselor, trying to find out why they keep falling for unattainable objects.

The point of your book should not be to show how the events you're describing affected you psychologically. Psychological explanations rob your characters of free will. If your book is about the injury done to you in childhood, well, the damage is done. Story over. If I tell you my father's mother died when he was five, and he was kicked from pillar to post, you will think you have the why of his story already. Everything he does afterward will be seen in the light of that injury—and thus viewed as inevitable. If he had no choices, there is no story.

The writer Marilynne Robinson, author of *Home* and *Gilead*, said that the therapeutic narrative is part of the "mean little myth" of our time: "One is born and in passage through childhood suffers from grave harm. The work of one's life is to discover and name the harm one has suffered." Don't fall for that "mean little myth." Remember, we want you to be a hero, not yet another writer denied the perfect parents, husband, and/or children she deserves.

While you're at it, avoid scenes in which you talk to a shrink (unless you're Tony Soprano, and even he got away with it only because he was a mob boss). If you need to relay the insights gained in a therapy session, you might instead shift those conversations to a sister or a friend.

And, please, no shrink jargon! Your mother did not suffer from financial abuse, she was robbed. No terms like *control freak, denial, validated*, or *passive aggressive*. No *closure* or *boundaries*. Be stingy with the words *realize* and *realization*. They can go limp and transparent after too much use. Dig around for other ways to say it.

Lastly, no dreams! You have a vivid dream life, and your dreams have often given you a deeper understanding of who you are. But dreams are not inherently dramatic—they didn't really happen, after all—and they are too personal. Use them only if essential.

THE CRAFTY WRITER

If you think your book is getting too psychological in a particular part, ask yourself, "Could I film this?" If you have pages and pages that contain nothing you could point a camera at, worry.

Do Your Research

Planning your memoir might include making some notes, doing some background research, even interviewing people who were part of the story. You may not use all of the resulting information, but it's enriching to have it.

Here's a useful step many writers skip: write down the important events of the book, and then the approximate dates on which they took place (day, month, and year—guess if you can't be sure). Add a sentence about what was happening in the world then. (Google is your friend here.) Keep a list of the birth dates of the people in your book handy so you know their age at any point.

With *Hold Me Close*, I knew my chronology would take Morgan from thirteen to seventeen. She was born in 1978, so my period was 1991 to 1996. With the second memoir I've been working on, about my father and my childhood, I started with the first date I could reliably remember: My sister Robin's birthday, May 9, 1963. She was conceived (simple subtraction tells me) the August before, in 1962, when my father came back from Mexico and he and my mother made a futile last stab at their marriage.

Knowing the dates tells you a lot—what was going on in the world at the time, how old everybody was, what headlines were in the news, what songs were playing on the radio, and so on. You can easily look any date up on the Web. I discovered that my father was turning forty at the end of the summer of 1961—a good fact to know if I am trying to figure out why he became so restless around that time.

You can also use historical background to widen the lens, so the narrative does not seem tightly focused on your states of feeling. Do some background reading, if necessary. To write a memoir about my childhood, I have to learn to think of my parents not just as people in the exciting lifetime role of being my parents but as people living in a certain time. That allows me to write comments that provided context, like explaining why my parents had so many kids so fast: "After the war, the whole country was obsessed with making babies, with hearth and home."

I collected a lot of books on the era (early sixties) that my unfinished childhood memoir is set in. I read *The Hot House: Life Inside Leavenworth Prison* to learn about the two years my dad spent in that storied federal slammer. My grandmother was a WAC (Women's Army Corps), so I got *Not All Soldiers Wore Pants*. Another book, *Homeward Bound: American Families in the Cold War Era*, gave me the perspective I needed on my parents' marriage, as did (to an astonishing degree) *Blue-Collar Marriage*.

INTERVIEW RELATIVES

Interviews can add interesting material to your book. Your memory is limited, and there may be events you don't remember, or weren't present at, that figure in your story. My brother Shannon turned out to have a crazy photographic memory. When I met him for dinner at an Italian restaurant in San Rafael, near the lumber company he manages, I had talked to older siblings and left him for last, as he is two years younger than I am. To my astonishment, he remembered everything about our childhood decades ago. "I can step out the front door of our old house," he said over his steaming lasagna, "and see it all, just like in a movie."

My brother told me a lot, including the saddest story I ever heard, about how when the shouting started between our parents, he'd go out and knock on neighbors' doors, one after the other, and get himself invited in. It was all the sadder for the expressionless way he told it, cutting his pasta and forking it in.

I interviewed my mother, too. She didn't much like talking about the old days, so I cleverly made a special appointment for the purpose. She couldn't *not* talk when I had driven twenty miles across the Golden Gate Bridge to her mobile home park in San Rafael just for the interview. (Also, when we went outside to sit at the rickety plastic table on her patio, I made a great show of setting out the tape recorder.) That day my mother told me, among other things, that she secretly bought a plot of land, and then sprung it on my father with the idea that he would build a house on it.

try this

Ask someone you trust to tell your story, either verbally or in writing. Perhaps some aunt or uncle or cousin would love to send you their recollections. This exercise can be amazingly illuminating for both you and the other participant. (Try not to bristle as your sweet old aunt remembers you as a spoiled layabout.)

CREATE SETTING

The setting of your memoir is the place where it happens, and the time it happens. Create a world for us. I know I like to be plunged into a world I don't know. Did you live on a rural dairy farm forty miles from San Francisco, at a time when that city was being rocked by the love revolution of the 1960s? Or did you grow up amid the tinkling of cocktail glasses in a tony suburb of Chicago? How did the setting affect you and the choices you made?

Here's the first paragraph of James Baldwin's *Notes of a Native Son*:

```
On the twenty-ninth of July, in 1943, my father died.
On the same day, a few hours later, his last child was
born. Over a month before this, while all our energies
were concentrated in waiting for these events, there
had been, in Detroit, one of the bloodiest race riots
in the century. A few hours after my father's funeral,
while he lay in state in the undertaker's chapel, a
race riot broke out in Harlem. On the morning of the
third of August, we drove my father to the graveyard
through a wilderness of smashed plate glass.
```

I think anybody reading that would agree that historical events contribute critically to the story Baldwin was telling.

Setting is anything that contributes to the sense of being in a particular spot on the planet at a particular time: the persistent fog, the wind in the trees, whether the landscape is open and rolling or bunched tight with towns hidden behind tall greenery. When you write about setting, think about how it affects your characters— are they comfortable in their space or ill at ease? A burg you long to escape from will be full of eyes, old-timey stores, and a movie theater that plays corny black-and-white movies. A town you left unwillingly will have friendly faces, a wonderful old five-and-dime, and a movie theater you could count on to screen *It's a Wonderful Life* for the entire month of November.

The writer Nora Johnson believes that we are profoundly affected by the places we have lived in, that every place changes us. The memories we carry of each place are not so much of the place itself as of ourselves when we were there.

Here's Frank McCourt providing the vivid setting for *Angela's Ashes*:

```
Above all, we were wet. Out in the Atlantic Ocean
great sheets of rain gathered to drift slowly up the
River Shannon and settle forever in Limerick. The rain
dampened the city from the Feast of the Circumcision
to New Year's Eve. It created a cacophony of hacking
coughs, bronchial rattles, asthmatic wheezes, consump-
tive croaks. It turned noses into fountains, lungs into
bacterial sponges.
```

Organize Your Material

You might drop your notes and other materials into baskets, one for each chapter, or event. Or keep a different-colored folder for each event (for example, "Mom's Wedding"). I also love the cardboard open file system, sold at places like Office Depot—so much easier than those hanging files in a drawer, the ones that are always slipping off their tracks.

Novelists often like to track a story by hanging a clothesline in an office, with the major scenes dangling on it, so they can see the whole book at once. Some people like to have a separate file for each chapter or section, but modern computers are so powerful that you can have the whole book in one file. Remember that in Microsoft Word, you can go to View and select Reading Layout to read the file in book format. Very handy, I've found.

For more tips on how to make the writing process a bit easier on the computer, see pages 241–242.

Write a Discovery Draft

Even as you're thinking about your story and gathering notes for it, you also want to write a lot of pages. Speed write. Go as fast as you can and the work will be authentic because you won't have time to censor. You might even do this in longhand, at a café, not at the computer. You won't have time to lie or to pull back from revealing. Your best work can come to the surface, your intuitive grasp of patterns and structures.

GO FORWARD, NOT BACK

Write, if you can, without worrying whether anyone will want to publish your ramblings or even read them, or even about whether your sentence has gotten really long and rambling and you want to go back and start it over and maybe take out the part about the whining and where are your images? Okay, that last sentence is a train wreck, but I'm not going to go back and read it. I'm just going to go on, because if I have learned anything, it's that writing is about going on.

Keep writing until you get tired of being nice. Write mean stuff. Write secret stuff. Go forward, not back, even if you realize that you had two children on page three and seem to have only one on page eight. It's satisfying to get at least a general shape of the story as it moves from beginning to end. You can even try to write the whole story in one short time period, using Red Bull or cappuccino or whatever drugs are handy.

E. L. Doctorow and others have compared creative writing to driving a car at night on a country road. You don't worry about anything but what is exposed in the glare of your headlights—the listing mailbox, the blur of a surprised deer, the glow of the gas gauge nearing empty on the dashboard. Writing this way has benefits: it keeps you from being overwhelmed by your task, and it forces you to slow down.

Don't try to fill us in. Don't look things up. Don't think about where to begin. Start with this phrase: "And another thing about . . ." If a memory surfaces—the sandy, sloping floors of a summer rental home, a pipe on a window sill, two horses drowsing with their heads close together—put that down, especially if strong feelings come up as you write.

You may have the urge to get out a cloth and shine up each sentence before you go on to the next one. But how do you know what sentences you'll keep when you haven't written the story to the end yet? If you keep stopping to fix things, the unconsciously brilliant writerly you—Jackson Pollack throwing pails full of paint onto the floor—will get pushed aside by the fussy little critic sniffing, "No one will want to see paint splatters. Look, it's all over your shoes."

Clustering is a handy exercise, first described by Gabriele Rico in *Writing the Natural Way*, that allows you to jot down ideas and make rapid connections between them. You write whatever you're working on in the center of the page, draw a circle around it, and then free-associate. I did this often when I was doing a column and wanted to rapidly generate new ideas. This technique works because you're not writing a sentence or a note, then going on to the next: You're all over the place, monkey mind—the way we think. With clustering, you catch all that. It sounds like a high-school exercise, but man, it works.

DON'T CENSOR YOURSELF

Don't worry at this stage what your mother will think when she reads this. In the first draft, put it all in. If you're writing each word with your mother looking over your shoulder, lips pursed, her sharp little fingers digging into your shoulder blades, you'll censor words you haven't even written yet. Blurt it all out. Later you can read through it to see what you've said about other people, and how it will make them feel to read it. (You may have to decide which you want: a published work or a mother who speaks to you.)

The main protection for your relatives is your own honesty in the writing. You write about other people, yes, but as I hinted above, you're the one screwing up, the one taking responsibility for what happened. If you attack other people, justifiably or not, the writing fails—because you're too angry or too much a victim or too unreflective. And if the writing fails, then you don't get your work published, and don't have to worry about people being mad at what you said in it.

eleven

WHAT GOES IN, WHAT DOESN'T

Just because it happened to you is no reason to write about it.
You have to be interesting or no one will care.

—STEPHEN DUNN

OKAY, YOU'VE done some preliminary noodling on your memoir.
You've accumulated pages of raw writing. Time to sit down and
bang it out?

Nope. Time to plan it. What goes in, and what doesn't? Where
does it start? Where does it end? (You don't want to bring it up to the
present.) If your story is about attending your mother in her last illness, and during that time you had a bout with bone cancer and met
a new man, are those events part of the story? How do you know?
What events will you minimize, which will you accentuate? Which
things—out of those that happened, those that you wanted to happen, and those that didn't happen—do you need to tell the story you
want to tell?

Identify Your Desire Line and Obstacles

I slogged along on early drafts of *Hold Me Close* for years. My friend
Donna Levin read a draft and said, "You have lots of material, you
know the story, and you write well. The problem is that the options

are so unlimited that you could keep arriving forever. The pile of papers will get bigger and bigger, but not more shaped."

WHAT DID YOU WANT?

In order to do that shaping, you need to realize that a memoir is a story and you are its hero. The first step is to answer that seemingly easy question: What did you want? This desire drives the main character, and thus it drives the book.

Playwright John Guare said, "I learned about playwriting from the jackets of show albums because I always noticed that the first or second song in any musical was the 'want' song—'All I Want Is a Room Somewhere.'" Think of the Yellow Brick Road gang in *The Wizard of Oz*: Dorothy wants to go home. The cowardly lion wants courage. The scarecrow wants a brain. The tin man wants a heart.

What did you want, in your story? You should be able to state it in a sentence:

```
I wanted my family to choose me over their religion.
I wanted to love my husband.
I wanted to be a pastor though I was already fifty-two.
I wanted to be the best damned stroke victim on the
    planet.
```

The desire must be one that makes the story about *you*. Don't hide behind your plot. Your desire shouldn't be "I wanted the school to accept my autistic son," but "I wanted to accept my autistic son."

In her book on writing memoir, *Your Life as Story*, my friend Tristine Rainer calls what you wanted in the story the *desire line*. The struggle to achieve the desire drives the book. (You might have heard fiction writers call it the *through line*.) The desire line may of course change by the end of the memoir. For example, a narrator who methodically engineers his own destruction may end by wanting to survive.

When I was writing the first drafts of *Hold Me Close*, I thought my desire line was "I wanted my daughter to be safe." The early drafts were an annotated list of Morgan's escalating escapades: "And then she cut class and lied and got in stolen cars with boys who went to other schools. . . . And then she met a boy who introduced her to speed and got her pregnant. . . . And she refused to go to the drug program and I kicked her out." In between each of her adventures, you were treated to shots of me sobbing on the bed or wetting her stepdad's shirt, the ocean air blowing in from the window Morgan had so recently disappeared out of.

I didn't even know that a memoir had to be about *me*. I had to keep searching until I got the right desire line, which was "I wanted to be a good mother."

Once you have your desire line, ask yourself additional questions:

```
What were my motives for wanting that?
How does the reader learn what I wanted? Through dia-
   logue? Actions? Interior thinking?
What actions did that desire set in motion? That is,
   what did I do to get what I wanted?
What or who stood in the way of achieving it?
What happened in the end? (Keep in mind that we learn
   about ourselves from what we don't get as well as
   from what we do get.)
```

You'll know when the desire line works, because it will give you the events of your book—what you did to get what you wanted, and what things got in your way. In a good memoir, you are an action hero. You try a lot of different things to solve your problem, have setbacks, make mistakes, and push on until you either get what you wanted or don't, or stop wanting it. You can begin outlining key events by jotting down a list of actions and obstacles:

```
I wanted _____.
I wanted it because _____ (backstory).
To get it, I _____ (action).
However, something got in my way: _____.
```

```
I had to try something different, so I _____. (There
    may be several action-reaction sequences.)
```

WHAT OBSTACLES GOT IN THE WAY?

What prevented you from getting what you wanted? (If the answer is nothing—you wanted X and X arrived that very morning—you don't have a book.) Obstacles are both external and internal: other people, adverse events, and most of all, ourselves—our illusions, passions, insecurities, vanity, pride, wanting the wrong thing. If the book is to be interesting, it should be about how you got in your own way, how you screwed up. Show us how your own actions and thinking made everything worse. What were your vulnerabilities? Your ego? Your romanticism? Your addiction to excitement? Your sense of entitlement? Your avidity for money? What were you afraid of, and how was that an obstacle to getting what you wanted?

Determine the Pivotal Events

Once you've thought about the desire line and the obstacles, you can start to identify the *pivotal events*—the happenings you know you must include in any version of the book no matter what. For example:

```
The day you discovered the bastard in bed with your
    best friend.
The day you decided to go to California.
The afternoon your son didn't come home from school.
```

Write the pivotal events (major turning points) first. Memoir writers often create a lot of scenes they later realize they don't need. This doesn't happen with pivotal events: they always go in.

IDENTIFY THE INITIATING INCIDENT

The most important pivotal event is the *initiating incident*. This is the event that forces you into the struggle of the book. Let me give you an example: My student Linda Curtis had a clear initiating incident in her memoir-in-progress about having to leave her religion (and her entire world) behind when her belief in Jehovah's Witnesses collapsed.

Before the trouble started, she was an unquestioning Jehovah's Witness. Then, on an ordinary Saturday morning, she was out knocking on doors, maybe peeved that her partner across the street was not doing as much as she should. Linda knocked on a door. A man in a faded college sweatshirt with a pair of gardening shears in his hand opened the door. It was not a stranger to be converted, but her boss from work, a man she admired and respected. He was as surprised as she was. He'd known she was a Jehovah's Witness, but now his star employee stood next to his porch swing with a copy of the *Watchtower* in her hand. Embarrassed, Linda had no choice but to go ahead with her spiel. She opened her mouth and out came the usual words, "The very existence of the intricately designed wonders in the universe surrounding us argues that an intelligent and powerful Creator produced it all . . ."

For the first time in Linda's life, the words sounded hollow to her own ears. Her trouble begins. Her struggle in the book is not to discard her religion but to hold on to it: to conquer these new doubts that will tear her from her belief system, her husband, her mother and father, and all she knows.

Your own initiating incident (called the *complication* in the short story) may be the day you stumbled on a walk across the college campus and realized that your desire for independence was being threatened by the worsening effects of your cerebral palsy. It might be the morning your mother referred to bananas as "those long yellow things," or the day you admitted your thinning child was not going to stop her obsessive dieting on her own. These initiating incidents are *always* dramatized in scene.

For another of my students, Frank, the trouble in his tale did not begin the day his estranged girlfriend, Diane, announced she was pregnant with his child. He figured that was her deal. He had never stood in a drugstore aisle puzzling over the numbers on the Huggies boxes and was not planning to. Out of a sense of duty, Frank showed up at the birth room at the hospital. He stood in back, ignored while everyone bustled around with monitors and beeping machines and chips of ice. After this, he thought, his part would be over. Then he saw his newborn daughter with her wet dark hair and tiny face, still a bit mushed from her ride through the tunnel, and just like that his shriveled bachelor's heart opened like a rose blooming in fast motion on the Discovery Channel.

The desire that will drive the book arrives like a jolt to his heart: No way is he going to miss out on being part of his child's life, ransacking shoe stores for the perfect jelly sandals, and hearing her say "Daddy" and mean him. Why is that trouble? Because when he arrives at his ex-girlfriend's condo with a teddy bear under his arm, she is distant and distracted. The nanny has been instructed to stay during his visit. And so begins a man's struggle to be part of his daughter's life—and his ex-girlfriend's determination that he will not.

In many stories there will be no single definitive initiating incident. If you have no specific incident that begins the trouble, you can sometimes use a prologue to create suspense. I did this in my memoir with a two-page prologue that consisted of a scene of my sixteen-year-old daughter, Morgan, packing. It included the lines, "She was not running away. I was throwing her out." (Looking back, I might have chosen as the initiating incident the night my daughter got in a car with two teenagers from a different school. That's when I realized she was making choices that could kill her, and I could do nothing to stop her. If I were writing the book again, I might start with her getting into that car.)

INCLUDE A STATUS QUO SCENE

Before the initiating incident, you will have a short *status quo scene*: The one that shows you in the midst of your ordinary life before the trouble starts. For example, in the memoir Linda is writing about losing her faith as a Jehovah's Witness, it could be a minor problem—perhaps she's grumpy about what side of the street she got. A status quo scene might show you fretting about a meeting as you swing your bike into a turn lane, just before you are struck from behind.

Nearly every movie begins with such a scene: the marriage before it ends, the child before she gets sick, the young spoiled German woman before she falls in love with the Jew hidden behind the stairs. In a story by my student Steve Jensen, a charter boat captain, he was served with divorce papers as his boat was leaving the dock in Sausalito, in full view of the passengers. In his status quo scene, just before the process server arrives, we see the ordinary problems of trying to please the tourists on board, a married man going about his work day.

The status quo scene must contain its own conflict so it will hold the reader's attention, but that conflict needn't be huge: If you're meeting your husband for the Friday dinner at which he'll disclose his illness, you can be fretting that the restaurant will run out of the smoked halibut you've been looking forward to all week, or hoping the new shirt you had monogrammed for him is ready.

Draw the Arc

As you identify what you wanted, and the actions you took to get it, and what and who got in your way, you are drawing the *arc* of your story. The arc outlines the emotional journey you take in the book, from start to finish: It's the plot of the memoir. Your status quo scene and the initiating incident will be at the beginning of your story arc.

The arc shows you the best place to begin. I started the story too far back in my own memoir. I wrote a hundred pages about Morgan in eighth grade. The people who read those pages yawned at my tales of a kid slamming doors, talking back, skipping school, and not speaking to me. "What's the big deal?" they said. "Every teenager is like this." I had to throw out months' worth of writing and start when the much bigger trouble started. An arc would have shown me that I was spending my emotional capital on little stuff—showing fury and fear and loss of confidence when my kid refused to study for a Spanish test. What would I have left to show when she was arrested?

The reason it's called an arc and not a straight line is that it represents an emotional *build*. Things must always get worse.

TRACE THE EMOTIONAL BEATS ON YOUR ARC

The arc maps the inner changes you undergo as you progress toward your goal. These are not just the events that happen in the book. They are descriptions of *the events combined with what emotions you were feeling at that point.* Each emotion that's acted on to move the story forward is a *beat* (thus events are also called beats). The event is always keyed to the emotion. Thus you would not say, "And then I went back to my wife," but "and then, with renewed determination to save the marriage for the sake of the kids, I moved back in with my wife."

Let's look at an example. A prosecutor in the New York City district attorney's office worked with me on a memoir about the year he spent in Kosovo as an international prosecutor. I've italicized the emotional beats. Imagine this drawn out on an arc:

Sam was a *bored and frustrated* lawyer in New York *wearily preparing* for yet another in a long line of red-on-blue Mexican gang crime cases. *He was good at what he did, and there was some pride in that, but he was often visited by a sense of futility.* There were a hundred DAs in Manhattan and cases would still get prosecuted if he were not around.

There was an opening for an international prosecutor in Kosovo (his initiating incident).

Excitement. He wants to go. He drives past his stop thinking about it.

The next day, he thinks, this is crazy — he can't go halfway across the world. He just got married and can't walk out on his life.

But he *can't stop himself* from doing research into the job. And it won't do any harm to fill out the application.

Surprise they say yes! *Elated*, he tells his boss.

Disappointment. His boss says he can't go or he'll be fired. Here's a big turning point: He now has to choose between the adventure job and his whole career. We see what he will lose if he quits his New York job.

Then a decision: *"Screw it, I want to go anyway."*

When he arrives in Pristina, the capital of war-torn Kosovo, which is being administered by the United Nations so the Serbs and Muslims won't return to killing one another, Sam is *filled with elation at his new sense of purpose*, until . . .

He discovers to his *dismay* that he will be the only international prosecutor in a region of roughly eight hundred thousand people. An impossible job is made harder by his unfamiliarity with the judicial system he has to use—one in which you can't even cross-examine witnesses. There is no functioning police force or judiciary. The place bristles with guns.

He realizes it's going to be hard to make a difference here, too. At his first trial, cops were shot at and victims were too terrified to testify. Other prosecutors have been killed.

Not only will he be unable to put war criminals behind bars, but he'll be lucky to get out alive himself.

Tempted to catch the next plane out, he thinks of his dad's heroics in World War II and *is filled with new resolve*. His father didn't quit.

Sam will stay, but now he is *just going through the motions, waiting out his time*.

> Then one day a man comes into the office with a story
> that *renews Sam's sense of purpose*.

And so forth. I am doing the complexity of his story a disservice here, as I am to all the stories I sketch in few words—I'm just trying to show how the combination of emotion plus event is what goes in the arc.

IDENTIFY THE BEAT, THEN CHOOSE THE EVENT TO SHOW IT

In his first beat, above, Sam needs to show how bored and useless he felt in his present job. How will he depict that? In any of several ways. Maybe a memo goes around, and there are one hundred names on it, reminding him that he is one of many people who can do this job. Maybe he remembers a time when he was sick or gone and it made no difference. Maybe we get not a scene but a montage—him appearing in the same courtrooms, in front of the same judges, year after year.

SIMPLIFY THE BEATS

In each beat, focus on one emotion. If the beat is that Sam is now just going through the motions until he can leave, we can't muddy that beat with all the other, contrary feelings human beings can hold in their heads at once: He's angry at the person who recruited him, he's falling in love with a coworker, he's discovering an interest in painting landscapes, and so on. It's not the job of writing to mirror life in all its complexity: that leaves the reader confused and overwhelmed, and he already has his own life to do that. The job of writing is to render the world and other human creatures understandable, and to show how the experiences of others can give us insights into our own behavior. Beats must be simplified, so that each event offers us one clear change.

SET UP THE BEATS

Remember setup, back in chapter 3? Ask yourself: Whatever I feel, what is the opposite? We can't have a series of scenes in which you tell us, in various ways, that your mother is going to die and you're upset about it. One beat: She's in a coma, but she's been in comas before!

She'll come out of it this time, too. That hope becomes the setup for the next beat, which is the end of that hope. Next beat, in new scene: See the color of mother's face or glimpse note on her chart that says, "prognosis poor." Realize she *is* going to die.

Don't bury important beats. If the scene is about you worrying that your adopted daughter might be handicapped, don't add, "We might end up regretting this decision. It could destroy us and our marriage," and then just leave that thought hanging as an unimportant afterthought.

Strengthen the Arc

I'm not going to tell you that deciding on the arc is an easy exercise, one that you can knock out in the half hour before dinner. It's not. Building an arc challenges you to survey the tangle of emotions, motives, repetitions, and complexities of events you lived through with the cold dispassionate eye of an editor; it requires you to select not what was important or meaningful to you, but what is important or meaningful to the *story*.

THROW YOUR BOOK ON THE FLOOR

I find it helps to put each event and its accompanying beat on an index card. One card, for example, might read: *Christmas with the folks: I see them simply and naturally accept my stepson as one of the family. Why can't I do that? What is wrong with me?* Lay all the cards out on the floor or on a table, get yourself a big glass of wine and a couple of undisturbed hours, and look them over.

Problems will arise as you study your cards, which is the whole point. Better to find and solve them at this stage, when they are still jottings on itty-bitty cards, than wait until you have hundreds of pages of polished manuscript that you have to toss to make the story work.

Ideally you want the event/beat on each card to lead neatly to the next. This won't happen. In real life, the day you realized your husband resented your getting sick is followed by something entirely unrelated, like the real estate deal you counted on fell through. Some events will need cutting (we got it that your ex was a swine—no need to insert the six scenes of additional evidence). Some will need moving. Some aren't there yet (you were not going to tell us that you lost your son's tuition in a Wheel of Fortune slot machine?).

As you pace up and down your row of cards, challenge each event's right to be there. At the same time, ask yourself how you reacted to the last event, and how does that lead into the next one? Make sure that each card contains the emotional intent of the scene, not just what happened. For example, not "We moved in with my mother," but "To hold the family together, I was even willing to move in with my mother."

ADD MISSING EVENTS

Your cards may reveal that events crucial to the book aren't yet there at all. Sometimes those will be the ones you couldn't face writing. That friend of mine I mentioned earlier, Connor, the young Irish drunk, gave us lots of pub scenes and lots of scenes with girls, but what we want, though it may be painful for him to write, is the scene in which he turns up on his wife's doorstep and takes fifty pounds from her. What have you left out? Make a list of possibilities.

Missing scenes might include events that never happened. Fantasies belong in autobiographical works as much as real events do—they show us what you're feeling, what you want, what you're afraid of. In *A Heartbreaking Work of Staggering Genius*, Dave Eggers shows how helpless he feels during his mother's illness by fantasizing a wild plan to get her out of the hospital with the help of his siblings, Beth and Toph:

```
We'll get her out in a few days. Beth and I have vowed
to get her out, have planned to break her out, even
if the doctors say no; we will hide her under a gur-
ney, will pose as doctors, will wear sunglasses and go
quickly and will take her to the car, and I will lift
her and Toph will provide some distraction if neces-
sary, something, a little dance or something; and then
```

```
we'll jump in the car and be gone, will bring her home,
triumphant . . .
```

I used fantasy briefly in *Hold Me Close* when I needed to show why I was determined to make Morgan do her homework:

```
I shook out Morgan's clown-sized overalls and folded
them into a square. I saw her, forty years old, in a
stained white blouse, hair lank across her forehead,
carrying five plates through a swinging metal door in
a restaurant because no one had made her do her home-
work in high school. I hadn't plucked the image out of
thin air: my mother had been forced to go to work as a
waitress after my father left. She came in tired, pasta
stains on her white blouse, and left slabs of leftover
tea cake and bags of French bread on the counter.
```

try this

Write a one-page fantasy in which you get whatever it is you want in the story you're telling. In a memoir of being a rebellious teen, the desire line might be "I wanted to destroy myself. My mother stopped me. My love of music stopped me. I realized I wanted a productive life." In the one-page fantasy of this, the writer might imagine his own funeral.

USE FLASHBACKS SPARINGLY

Flashbacks—or backstory—may or may not be vital. Remember what Holden Caulfield said in *Catcher in the Rye*:

```
If you really want to hear about it, the first thing
you'll probably want to know is where I was born, and
what my lousy childhood was like, and how my parents
```

```
were occupied and all before they had me, and all that
David Copperfield kind of crap, but I don't feel like
going into it, if you want to know the truth.
```

A good general rule: Don't pull the reader out of the narrative to tell what happened in the past unless it's for a good reason. Flashbacks must add to the emotional complexity of what's going on in the present. You got your tubes tied when you were sixteen, but in a memoir the reader doesn't need to know it until the scene where you meet Bill Gates and he wants kids.

Say you want to show yourself, in the story, an exhausted single mother, ignoring the pile of bills on the coffee table and the smell of pot from your teenagers' bedroom, though both should be dealt with. Do you need your memory of your mother and her friends giddily smoking grass in the kitchen when you were ten? No. It *seems* related—there is pot in both scenes—but is it? If a flashback can come out without hurting the story, then it has to come out. We understand why an overwhelmed mother might put off dealing with the smell of pot: We don't need a childhood memory to explain it to us. When in doubt, take it out.

Use of flashbacks also depends on your story. If you're writing about a stroke that came unexpectedly, you don't need events leading up to it (except to show the status quo): a stroke is a freak occurrence. If you're writing about being a bad father, however, flashbacks of your parents may be important.

I loved the way my student Casey sneaked this flashback about her husband into her memoir:

```
Julian looked up at me, a half-smile crossing his lips.
An outsider might think he was fighting back a grin,
but I knew better. Julian wasn't laughing. He felt
helpless, the same way he had felt helpless when I
walked into the bar that afternoon where he sat hunched
over a glass of scotch, after he told me he'd been
sober for a year. The same half-smile had crossed his
```

```
lips in that moment, when, four months pregnant with
Patti, I picked up the glass, poured the scotch over
his head and walked out. I had gone home alone. Julian
stayed away for a time after that, one night, two
nights. How long had it been? And I had cried all the
while, letting loose my sobs, pounding the floor, curs-
ing him for his weakness and deception, cursing myself
for my foolish gullibility.
```

The arc and the cards should help you see what belongs in the story and what doesn't. With memoir, you need such help. At least with fiction you know what to put in and what to leave out: If there's a car crash in a tulle fog, it's there because you need it. You made it up. In a memoir, the car crash may have nothing to do with the story, but it was such an explosive event that it may take several drafts to see that you don't need it.

DON'T INCLUDE *EVERYTHING*

If you put in everything that happened, the result will be an *episodic plot*, one in which no event is really more important than any other: the climatic scene of the mother leaving the house with a suitcase gets no more space than the long scene at a party with a boyfriend in which nothing much changed.

Remember murdering your darlings back in the chapter on revision? It **really** applies here in a memoir, where so much crowds in— your whole life, everything that was going on at the time. We need the scene in the shower when your right arm went limp, but do we need the ambulance trip? It was a joyous time when you brought your Chinese orphan home and the whole neighborhood came over to meet her, but did anything change? If not, mention the party in narration and go on. I had a scene in my memoir-in-progress of my dad carrying goat feed home on the bumper of his car after the store owner said it would fall off (it did). I loved that scene, but eventually had to admit it was not essential to the story.

Why It's Called Creative Nonfiction

I don't want to shock you, but Thoreau collapsed his two years at Walden Pond into one. Most autobiographical writers know that the *emotional truth* (how it felt to you) is more important to the story you're telling than the *literal truth* (what day it was, exactly what your brother said, whether or not it really was raining that day). What *happens* is fact. Truth is *how we react to what happens*. You are, after all, not just remembering: you are updating the past, sifting through it, even giving us several ways to view one event.

To remember is partly to imagine: It's a creative act. That's why it's called creative nonfiction.

You can't reproduce life exactly as it is—it would take thousands of sentences to describe taking a sip of coffee, and even then you would have to leave something out, like the weight of the coffee cup in your hand and the particular way you use your thumb to counterbalance it. To write anything down, anything at all, is to select from among possibilities, to choose the blue shirt and leave the red shirt forever at the back of the closet.

All of which is to say, that sometimes you will need a scene, as my student Adele did, to show a turning point in her mother's life:

> I watched Mother slip off her gloves, and I tried to imagine her as the eleven-year-old girl on a ship coming to America from Russia. I could see her as she slipped away from her mother and came up to the deck, clutching a piece of paper. She held the paper over the swirling water then pulled her hand back close to her body. Before Mother left Russia, her friend, Pupil, had given her the note with her name and address and asked my mother to deliver it to my father to be. My mother brushed her wind-blown hair with her hand and argued with herself: "I promised Pupil, but I want Isadore for myself. I must make him like me." She dropped the note into the ocean.

Of course Adele was not there when her mother was an eleven-year-old on a ship. You have to use your imagination.

And you have to consider the reader's needs. If over the course of six weeks your boyfriend makes six pissy remarks about the new dog, by all means put them in one conversation. Patricia Hampl told the magazine *Writers Ask*: "If you read *Virgin Time* you would say I went to Italy only once. In fact, I traveled to Italy over a period of five years, taking five or six trips, and using parts of them to create one journey in the writing. Much of what happened, whole summers of experience, didn't fit the questions at the center of the book. So what is that, suppression of the truth?"

Hire an Editor

If you're at work on a book, consider hiring a professional to help you think it through. The editor won't be overwhelmed by the avalanche of real events that crowd your memories, all desperate to be included: She will know what the story needs. Many published writers credit their breakthroughs to hiring one of the many talented editors (sometimes called book doctors) that the economy and the consolidation of publishing has washed out of New York publishing houses. Many of these editors advertise their services in the back pages of *Poets & Writers* magazine.

I hired several people at various times to read the manuscript of the book in your hands, in addition to strong-arming my husband and friends into it. One editor, Judith, pronounced the draft she read to be "not a manuscript but a compilation of ideas, anecdotes, and quotations from yourself and other authors." Her comments went on for pages. I flushed as I read them. I cursed Judith and her ancestors and the horse she rode in on. I sent her feedback to friends saying, "Can you *believe* this?" They loyally assured me that Judith was a Nazi, and said not to pay attention to her.

And then I calmed down. And read Judith's comments carefully, rewrote, and made the book much better.

Then I made it worse again, restoring darlings, moving things around. (Tell me you haven't done this yourself.)

I finally asked my sister Robin to read it, and she turned out to be the perfect reader, willing to ask the dumb questions and tell me when I was being "lofty" (her word). She not only let me know which chapters were slow but how to fix them. She lavishly admired what she liked, which helped me accept what she didn't.

An editor, like a writing partner, sees only what is in front of him: what works, what doesn't, what's missing, what you said before, and so on. And unlike friends, an editor is trained at proposing solutions and at reading manuscripts analytically. An editor doesn't just identify problems: he has an idea how to fix them.

As the novelist Michael Crichton said:

> You generally start out with some overall idea that you can see fairly clearly, as if you were standing on a dock and looking at a ship on the ocean. At first you can see the entire ship, but then as you begin work you're in the boiler room and you can't see the ship anymore. . . . What you really want in an editor is someone who's still on the dock, who can say, "Hi, I'm looking at your ship, and it's missing a bow, the front mast is crooked, and it looks to me as if your propellers are going to have to be fixed."

According to the Brenner Information Group, it takes, on average, 475 hours to write each draft of a fiction book, and 725 hours for a nonfiction book. A good writing coach can save you a whole draft of a book in a couple of hours, just by going over your plot with you. If someone saves you a draft, she saves you 725 hours.

THE CRAFTY WRITER

Working with a paid editor helps long before you even meet with him or her. When a woman emailed me to ask if I could edit her work, we set up an in-person consultation. She later told me that she spent all weekend getting ready for our meeting—and thought about her book so much that she'd made a lot of progress in the three days since she'd emailed me.

Consider a Nonconventional Structure

We've been talking thus far about a memoir that follows the conventional dramatic structure of a story. I should not end the chapter without noting that a memoir can offer meditative and impressionistic examinations of self, rather than a straightforward story. It's an elastic form, after all. You can move back and forth in time, as in Philip Roth's *Portnoy's Complaint* (billed as a novel, I know, but a memoir all the same, like almost all his stuff). You can gather remembered fragments that gain a coherence of their own. Such memoirs serve theme rather than event. Sven Birkerts, in *The Art of Time in Memoir*, describes memoir as a circular genre: "Each is in its own way an account of detection, a realized effort to assemble the puzzle of what happened in the light of subsequent realization."

The writer—and the reader—fills in strategic blanks with surmises and imaginings, in a book that can seem almost like collage. The result can be more lyrical, more poetic, than novelistic. *Safekeeping* by Abigail Thomas is, as my student Kris Seeman said, "Not so much memoir as a stained glass window of scenes of a grown-up woman who has learned to rejoice in being herself. Reading it, we feel the crazy beauty of life."

Your memoir can take the form of a search for patterns and connections that explain you to yourself, that give your life and your past new meaning. You surprise yourself in the process—the events that have always been up there in the marquee of your memory may turn out not to be the important ones.

The risk with collage is that while it looks temptingly simple—much as an abstract expressionist painting might to a student painter—it is not. An intuitive calibration of effects must supply the sense of unity that would otherwise be supplied by story. You must repeat images, colors, patterns—something for the reader to recognize and track. And the less headlong narrative there is, the more engaging the voice must be, the more arresting the images.

try this

Read one acclaimed memoir and think about the decisions the author was making as she wrote. Why does she begin—and end—where she does? What is left out? How much is in scene, how much in narrative? Why was this book published?

You'll notice that I often refer to the "events" in your book when talking about the arc. These events can be dealt with on the page in one of two ways: in narration, or in scene. Some memoirs, such as *Angela's Ashes*, are almost all scene; others, such as Vladimir Nabokov's *Speak, Memory,* are almost all narration. More and more, however, modern memoirs use scenes to make a book lively and readable.

In the next chapter, we turn to exactly what a scene is and how to write one—and also to the power of good narration.

twelve

HOW TO WRITE NARRATION AND SCENE

Storytelling reveals meaning without committing the error of defining it.

—HANNAH ARENDT

Although most of us are pretty good at narration, writing a scene is a distinct skill, and you will have dozens of them in a typical memoir. In this chapter we'll devote some time to finding out exactly what scene and narration are—a subject that leads us naturally to dialogue and characters, the people in your book who will be moving through those scenes and speaking that dialogue.

The Uses of Narration

Narration, also called "summary," is the writing in between scenes, in which you pull the camera back, cover ground quickly, or reflect and offer perspective. Here's an example of narration from my student Chris Voisard:

```
It wasn't as if I slowly drifted away from liking
the good boys. I made a conscious decision one day
```

while I was taking a shower. Before that day, I loved
smart, straight-A kind of boys. In seventh grade,
I fell in love with Jay Alves, the best player on the
basketball team, the only team sport played at Cunha
Junior High . . .

When I was working on *Hold Me Close,* I didn't quite have the knack of narration down. I was so happy to have learned how to write a scene that the book was practically a play. My first editor at Random House, Harriet Bell, said in a letter: "You take far too long to get to the gist of the story. While some of the escapades, lies, and details are important, it would move things along if you summarized the daily grind of living with Morgan. The retelling of everything Morgan did makes it difficult to separate the annoying stuff from her really heinous actions."

I had to learn to use narration to move faster, as in "The second half of Morgan's freshman school year and the first half of her sophomore year passed in a haze of arguments, stalemates, and outbursts."

When my friend Darlene was working on a memoir, she told me:

I naturally thought I needed to put in every awkward
lesbian love scene. They were some of my most candid and precious moments. I thought, "They will love
it, it's real, sexy kinda, and develops my character."
But really, after the first one or two I should have
said, "I continued to choose women who turned out to be
straight for the next six years before I wised up."

She learned to avoid emotionally repetitive scenes—scenes that give us a different example of something we already know. You dramatize something once, and put similar events in summary: "This became a pattern over the next year."

Write Compelling Scenes

Narration allows you to speed through time, to cover events you need that aren't important enough to fully dramatize, and to offer the reader the reflective voice we talked about in chapter 10. A *scene*, in contrast, is an event that takes place in real time on the page. If the narration is the string, the scenes are the pearls. Something significant happens in every scene, something that has not happened before in the story and will not happen again. A scene can be of any length, from a few lines to twenty pages (though in general, the more impor-tant the scene, the more space it should take up). It's one in a sequence of distinct events that moves the story toward the end. In a memoir, you might have fifty scenes interspersed with narration.

The good news? If you can write one scene, you can write those fifty scenes. If you can write fifty scenes, you can write a book.

The question is, *can* you write a scene? I mentioned how happy I was to have learned what a scene was and how to write one that I got carried away and had too many scenes. Too many scenes is as bad as too few, because a scene signals the reader that this is impor-tant stuff—and it can't all be important stuff. A story's pace slows when the unimportant (the trip to Mt. Whitney or meeting a friend who will soon disappear from the narrative) gets as much emphasis as the important (the parents' obliviousness to the narrator's worsening drinking problem, for example).

STEP ONE: IDENTIFY IMPORTANT EVENTS FOR SCENES

So your first step is to identify which events are important enough to go into a scene. In the last chapter, we saw that each emotion that's acted on to move the story forward is a beat. Beats are changes, thus they are dramatized: All important changes must be dramatized in scene. If we see you doing something you would not have done before, we want to be there with you when that change occurs. If something happens one night to make you realize that you are not the freak you took yourself to be, show it. If you feed your once-scary father yogurt with a spoon in the hospital, and feel a new kind of love for him, show it.

Each time something happens that produces a change in you, you drop into scene to show it. Here are some examples:

```
When you realize that you can't face one more day at
    the job you've held for years
When you get the diagnosis
When you watch the video of the kids in the wading pool
    and realize your daughter is deaf
When you're working up the nerve to ask your husband
    for a divorce but he asks you for one first
```

These moments are the *hot spot* in the scene—the moment of change. A scene has a little arc of its own: from hope to despair, or from frustration to having a plan. Your overriding desire in the book may be to become a mother, say, but there's also a series of smaller desires that push you along in each scene—to talk your husband into it, to force him into bed when the thermometer says it's a good time, and so on.

Sometimes your hot spot is subtle, shown largely in action (someone not answering a question, leaving a room). Other times it will be stated outright. In his memoir, *This Boy's Life*, Tobias Wolff remembers when his new stepfather, with whom he has a contentious relationship, leaves him alone in the car. The formerly rebellious young Wolff thinks, "I didn't want to get in more trouble. I wanted everything to go right." That's a change, that last sentence. Scene over.

Start a scene as late in the action as you can and get out right after the change.

STEP TWO: DRAMATIZE THE SCENE

The second step is learning to do the step-by-step imaginative labor of dramatizing a scene. When I started out, my idea of a scene was to park my character on a bench and have her think back. You might do this too, because it's easier to talk about what happened, how you felt about it, and all that than it is to dramatize what happened.

Also, you know so much about the backstory—since the event happened to you—that it often wants to come tumbling into the scene. Say you begin with a sentence that puts us firmly in scene: "Mary strode into the bar and spotted her husband with his ex-wife." We want to see what happens next in the bar, but instead hear, "What a rat. After I had put him through dental school. My mother was right . . ." and so on. Swinging into backstory or commentary is more comfortable than staying in the room with your character and getting her across the bar floor. Whenever you start to enjoy the writing, stop and ask yourself, Am I blathering on?

DO YOUR COMMENTING BETWEEN SCENES

Notice, in this rough draft by a student, how much is commentary (in italic) and not scene at all:

> *I thought the worst part of my first medical checkup in a couple of years was going to be Dr. Carr's index finger reaching up my butt looking for nuggets or polyps or something else. It's not an abnormal fear of a gloved hand that has kept me away, rather the good doctor's guidance that an annual physical wasn't necessary for a man of my age.* But, as I sit, waiting, in the corner of a small examining room, wearing this Bounty paper towel, *it's hard to argue that "not every year" equates to one every five years. Is there even a word for that?* Carr, a seasoned, stooped man with a kind, professorial manner, greets me warmly. *The first time I saw him was back in January, six months before, when my back seized up during an early morning run. He'd told me to gobble down Advil like they were M&Ms. On my own, I pushed up into downward facing dog at the yoga studio, pulled down weights on the lat press machine, and allowed myself to be manipulated (albeit at the chiropractor's office).*

Imagine if you were watching a movie and they froze the frame and starting talking to you like that. You can—must!—have reactions in a scene, but keep them short and pertinent to what's happening. Writer Casey Simon does this in a scene from her memoir-in-progress, in which the ex-husband and the narrator try to coax an anorexic daughter to eat. I've put the narrator's thoughts in italic:

"Patti, you've got to eat," Julian said. His voice was firm. *I could see the simple 'JF' embroidered on the cuff peeking out from the sleeve of his suit jacket. Julian Filatreau. It was one of his custom shirts, the ones he had specially tailored to fit his long body. He hadn't always worn custom shirts.*

I waved him off, forcing a smile. *I knew he felt bad, even responsible, in his mother-hen kind of way. I knew he genuinely wanted to help, but in this moment I couldn't think of a single thing he could do, except go away.* He had a sandwich on a plate in his hand; his lunch—tuna mixed with plain yogurt instead of mayonnaise, on a toasted whole-wheat bagel. *It was the lunch he ate most days.* I watched him disappear into the bedroom. *Maybe if I left them alone, Julian could get through to Patti. Maybe he could do what I had not been able to do: make her eat, make her laugh; make her forget whatever it was that had thrown her into this annihilative abstinence.* "I'll go change," I said then. "I'm not going back to the office today anyway."

Notice that Casey avoids commentary that takes us out of scene. She doesn't write sentences such as "I remembered six years ago when she was in the Brownies."

MORE TIPS ON SCENE

1. You can transition from narration into scene by saying something like, "And then one day . . ."
2. You might also find yourself going from *continuous action* (what always happens) in narration to scene: "Most mornings I got out of bed and went straight to my writing desk where I'd stored a thermos of coffee the night before." Then: "One day I found my husband sobbing in my chair."
3. You don't always have to give us transitions between scenes. Just hit the space bar a couple of times and jump into the next

one. If your character pops up at the office party, we can take for granted that she got there somehow—no need for us to drive along with her.

4. At the end of the scene, try for a dramatic curtain line—"Yes, I slept with her!"—that will push us into the next page. (It's a good idea to have one at the end of chapters, too).

5. The more important the scene is, the more image and detail it gets. After all, when you watch a horror movie, the camera doesn't zip straight to the kitchen to show the pills scattered on the linoleum and the woman in a bathrobe slumped across the dinner table. It goes first to the hallway closet, then creeps down the hall, then lingers on a burning cigarette in an ashtray, then lets us hear a siren in the distance. If your readers missed something that is right there in the story—you said your father was holding a pistol—you didn't use enough detail to slow down the narrative and draw attention to the gun.

try this

Let's practice writing a short scene. Who's in this scene? You, for sure. How old were you? What do you want? What's keeping you from getting it? What's at stake? Write ten images of people, ten quotes, five images of time and place. Locate us in time and space. What was happening in the world at that time?

QUESTIONS FOR THINKING ABOUT A SCENE IN YOUR MEMOIR

Instead of just launching into the writing of a scene, you can take some time to think about it and even jot some notes as you do so. Here are some important questions to ask yourself:

    What is the event in your scene? Does something clearly
      happen?
    What do you want in the scene?
    What's keeping you from getting it?

Where's the best place to set the scene? Is the scene
   grounded in time and place?

How do you respond to what happens?

Is your response all interior, or is there action?

What's the mood of the scene?

What changes in the scene, and how does that move the
   story forward?

How does this scene connect with the one behind and the
   one ahead?

Is the event important enough to be a scene, or could
   you just summarize it and leave it at that?

What's the purpose of the scene? This could include
   conveying information, a confrontation, a decision, a
   revelation, turning point, capitulation, resolution.
   Can you summarize this purpose in a sentence?

Is it clear where the scene begins and ends?

Do blocks of flashback or commentary or description
   break up the flow?

Can you enter the scene at a later point?

Check: for every action, is there a response?

try this

Is your memoir on the short side? Here's an exercise you can repeat as often as you need: Find an emotional sentence in a piece
and expand it into a short scene. (Make it a loaded sentence, like
this one: "The first time my mother had asked me if I was experi-
encing those symptoms again, I was not ready to talk about it.")

Bring Your Mom to Life

In a scene, the action unfolds right in front of us—we hear your characters, see their gestures, and smell their cigar smoke. That means scenes
provide a good way to sneak in description and characterization—why

say your sister is greedy when you can show her taking more than her share of cookies?

Whether you put those revealing details in narration or scene, keep in mind that when your mother appears in your memoir, she is not your mother, but a character. So are you, for that matter. You can't completely transfer the real Mom from your childhood kitchen to the pages of your book; she's far too complex to be fully captured in a few hundred pages. However, you can still make your mother a vivid character by including details, actions, and dialogue that bring her to life.

FIND BEHAVIOR THAT REVEALS YOUR CHARACTERS

Find the eccentric behavior that shows us how someone is different from everybody else. One student wrote, "My father bought whatever was on sale, a half-dozen lime green Burberry men's rain hats with yellow stitching on them or a two-pound tin of Galloping Gourmet ground paprika."

Collect details that reveal character. My dad was a contrary sort—in high school he ignored most assignments, but when a teacher said it would take all spring to memorize "The Raven," he did it overnight. You might mention that your mother polishes her nails only once for a wedding, then takes the polish off. Here's a revealing tidbit from a student: "My mother had a habit of cutting up a good likeness of herself and superimposing it, gluing it, on another not quite as flattering."

When you say, "My mother was home," give us images so we know whether to picture an Argentine matron polishing her hall mirror, or a Louisiana nurse's aide passed out in front of *Judge Judy* with an empty bottle of Gilbey's in her hand. (I seem to be picking on moms, don't I?)

One of my students described a roommate like this:

```
I knew immediately that Hank, for one, would be right at
home, because as soon as he arrived he kicked off his
shoes and dropped his wet jacket on the floor. He ac-
cepted my offer of orange juice with alacrity and later
padded into the kitchen in fuzzy turquoise socks to help
himself and Susan to more, plus a shot of my tequila.
```

Don't forget to sketch yourself. In first-person novels, there's famously a point on about page three where the protagonist catches sight of herself in a shop window or something, so the author can describe her. More adroitly, you can choose a situation where the narrator might feel self-conscious ("I could feel him looking at the place on my skirt where I'd spilled the wine"). You can show yourself nervously choosing what to wear or noticing a change ("My usually thick mane of hair had thinned . . .")

One student wrote, "When I'm home and not expecting company, I usually wear a T-shirt and shorts. Sometimes just the T-shirt. When I am expecting company, I am likely to add my pearl earrings and the shorts for sure."

What people say shows who they are as well. In her memoir, *The Facts of Life*, Maureen Howard writes:

> "Ah, did you once see Shelley plain," one of my mother's beloved lines, delivered on this occasion with some irony as we watched Jasper McLevy, the famed Socialist mayor of Bridgeport, climb down from his Model A Ford.

That's the way to quickly sketch your mother. A mother who ironically quotes Browning on seeing the mayor isn't everybody's mother—she's a particular person. What did your own mother say? Here are some students' responses to that question:

> "Nice girls don't jiggle," Mom informed us as we obligingly, with the help of a liberal dash of baby powder, forced ourselves into Playtex girdles. (Cheri Doege)

> "You look like a fullback," my mother said when I put on the dress. (Carol Costello)

> "I love you way too much to send you to summer camp," said my mother. "Only parents who do not love their children and want to be rid of them send them off."

THINK ABOUT YOUR REAL-LIFE CHARACTERS THE WAY
A FICTION WRITER THINKS ABOUT HIS INVENTED ONES

Make lists of (1) what you know about the character and (2) how you know it. Another very good exercise is to compile a detailed, specific list of five "loves," "hates," "wants," and "always" (habitual actions) for major characters, and in each case say *why*. We respond to characters when we know what they feel intensely about.

Here, just as an example, are some jottings from the lists I've created about my parents for my childhood memoir:

```
MY FATHER LOVES:
1.  Camping out. Why? He said of himself, "I need an
    aridity of circumstance to feel good about myself."
2.  Working with his hands. He once built a boat from
    plans in a magazine and invented a better plumb
    bob. Why? It was a creative outlet for him in a
    life that cast him otherwise as unsuccessful hus-
    band, unsuccessful father.
3.  Being funny. He was his own best audience. He said
    his dream was to have someone walk off after he
    finished talking, then suddenly get the joke and
    crack up. Why? He wanted attention and didn't get
    enough of it as a carpenter living and working in a
    rural valley.


MY FATHER HATES:
1.  Being indoors. Why? Because he spent two years at
    Leavenworth prison.
2.  TV. Why? He said it was for morons.


MY FATHER WANTS:
People to see he wore the clothes of a working man, and
see it as a sort of poetic, Thoreau-ian choice. Why? He
wanted to feel as though he mattered—to other people,
but mainly to himself.
```

```
MY MOTHER ALWAYS:
Went to the library and took out the maximum allowed,
usually biographies. Why? She was dissatisfied with
her own life and sought refuge in the lives of other
people.
```

try this

Write a how-to guide for someone undertaking an impersonation of the character, that is, how to be Dad (or whomever). What are this person's characteristic physical gestures?

Write out seven to ten very personal questions, then interview characters in your book using these questions. Write down the answers they give you, in their own words. (These answers may easily become short monologues or bits of dialogue in your published pages.)

Here's a paragraph from a student paper that captures a father at dinner:

```
Once during a meal Pop raised his eyes from the paper
and pointed across the table to some cheese he wanted
to put on his bread. My oldest brother, then nine-
teen years old, said to my father, "It has a name."
The rest of us trembled inwardly with fear. You just
did not dare to make a remark like that to Pop. Phew,
such luck. Raising his right eyebrow a bit, Pop said,
"Kaas," (cheese in Dutch) without a "please." My
brother passed the cheese to Pop without a word, but
I saw the twitch of a little smile at the corner of
my father's lips.
```

Use Dialogue

"Dialogue is what people do to each other." I can't remember where I read that, but to me it says give us conflict in the discussion, not chitchat. Readers won't put up with two old friends chatting, like this:

> "Hey, glad you could make it. Coffee?"
> "Yes, that would be nice."

Dialogue is readable, makes writing move fast, and it provides the fastest way to reveal character. There are two main kinds, *direct* and *indirect*:

> DIRECT DIALOGUE: "I'll back the car out," John said.
> INDIRECT DIALOGUE: John said he'd back the car out.

You can combine direct and indirect dialogue. For instance:

> They argued about who was going to back the car out (they were both a little drunk), and then John said, "I'll back it out."

Even in a heated exchange between two speakers, keep putting in *dialogue tags* that tell us where they are and what they're doing so they don't become disembodied voices. In the exchange below, the dialogue tags are in italic.

> "I don't care what you do anymore," John said. *He rinsed his coffee cup under the kitchen tap and was gone.*
>
> "Fine," Mary said softly *to the sound of his truck roaring down the gravel driveway.* "Neither do I."

Avoid great blocks of dialogue. We're not allowed to say much before we're interrupted by others or by something else going on. Cut out the extra words that clutters real speech ("Well" and "You know"). You don't need people to *whine*, *whimper*, *sneer*, *growl*, and—ugh!—

enthuse or *quip*. It's fine to keep repeating, "he said," because the eye skips right over it.

DON'T FORGET THE SUBTEXT

Dialogue gets interesting when there's *subtext*, what characters are really saying between the lines. Subtext is the unspoken thoughts and motives of characters, what they really think and believe. Remember Woody Allen's movie *Annie Hall*, in which subtitles give you the characters' thoughts as opposed to what we hear them saying?

My student Barbara Cressman opens a piece about her dissolving marriage with this nice paragraph of subtext:

> The pale sun worked its way between the leafless branches of the persimmon tree and filtered into the dining room through the tall patio doors. It was January 8th, 1984. There were two half-filled coffee cups on the old round table, plus a couple of our little Dansk plates, dotted with toast crumbs. Today was the day that Pete was going to move out on his own. He had lots to do, but then, so did I.
>
> "I'll iron your shirts," I said, all cheery.
>
> "Oh, Barb, you don't have to do that," said Pete, with a kind of pleading look on his face.
>
> "Well, you have to have nice shirts to wear to work!" I set up the ironing board and gathered an armful of several of his pretty, stripey shirts. I put some water into the steam hole of the iron. I also sprinkled the shirts with the old wine bottle that wore a little metal sprinkler top. He'd be out on his own and it was important for him to look okay.

The narrator here doesn't say how she feels about her husband's leaving, but it's there, in her insistence on doing something for him, one last time. "It was important for him to look okay," she says, but that's not the real reason she's ironing his shirts, is it?

"I'll iron your shirts," could be translated, "I am heartbroken, and it will soothe me to do this one last wifely thing."

"Oh, Barb, you don't have to do that!" could be read as, "I feel like hell already, and it pains me to see you wanting to do something nice for me."

In her memoir-in-progress, *Wicked Stepmother*, Erika Johnson includes a conversation between her and her stepson's mother about whether Erika will attend a school function:

> Sally says, "You don't need to worry about coming. It's really not necessary. I'll be there." (Subtext: *You aren't his mother and I don't want you acting in that role.*)
>
> "He asked me to come and I'm happy to do it," I reply. (Subtext: *I don't want to do it either, but he wants me there. Why are you sabotaging my relationship with him?*)

try this

Write two pages in which there is subtext—for instance two people are talking amiably but are really furious (maybe they had a fight the night before and are now at breakfast pretending all is okay).

All of these elements we've been talking about—narration, scene, vivid characterization, and dialogue—make a memoir a lively read. Scenes allow readers to be right there in the room, seeing what happens. Narration gives us the author's voice (it is here where you often find reflective voice) and moves us vividly and quickly through time. It is no coincidence that these are the elements borrowed from that staple of readerly delight, the novel. This is what the reading public is looking for, after all—a pleasurable literary experience. And readers, of course, are what every writer wants. In the next two chapters, let's talk about how to get the pages you've worked so hard on, whether essays or memoir, into the hands of those readers.

PART V

GETTING

PUBLISHED

thirteen

WORDS FOR MONEY
Selling Your Essays

No man but a blockhead ever wrote, except for money.

—SAMUEL JOHNSON

NOTHING BEATS a byline for a solid rush. I first felt that rush at eighteen. My local paper, the *Marin Independent Journal*, held a contest for the best comments on the generation gap and published the winners over a number of days. Inspired by the fact that they printed my sister Nora's effort, in the eighteen-to-twenty-one age category, I cribbed notes in the College of Marin library and scribbled something about how weird our parents were about money after growing up during the Depression (people who won't even pick up prescriptions if they decide they cost too much). The paper printed it and gave me a prize of $125. It was the first money I made from writing, and it allowed me to go hitchhiking in Europe that summer. My name in that paper, not to mention my name on that check, was like what an addict must feel shooting up: How soon can I feel this again? What must I do?

Of course—and this is an inconvenient fact—I did have to *send my piece to the paper* before the paper could accept it. The editors who publish essays—on the Web, or in newspapers or magazines—won't break into your living room, fall on their knees, and demand to be allowed to publish your work. It's unfair, but they don't. You must find their address or their email, study the spelling of their name, attach your document or paste it in, and then press Send (or stick a stamp on the envelope and put it in the outgoing mail).

I know. It's like going out of your way to ask people to be mean to you. You write fifty drafts of the heart-stopping story of how you and your brother were reconciled at last in a seaside bar at five in the morning, putting the last and finest draft in the mail—perhaps even walking out to the mailbox on the corner so the mailman doesn't lose it among his fistful of red Netflix mailers. And you get back (eventually) not the tearful acceptance you would prefer ("Is it true that you will allow us to publish this beautiful work?") but a Xeroxed note saying, "This doesn't meet our needs at this time." That is, if you get a response at all.

Why run into the street knowing the odds are good that you will be flattened by a truck? If you don't show your work to editors, they have no chance to not like it. Maybe a better idea is to keep it in a drawer, or show it only to those special someones (your children, perhaps, or Mom) who can be depended on to exclaim over it. That way, you can warm yourself at the fire of your genius undisturbed.

Does that sound cowardly? Maybe do this instead: Mail a piece to the hardest magazine in the country to break into. When it's rejected, give up on being published. My friend Tanner, a bank vice president, wrote a piece about his boyhood in Mississippi and sent it to the *New Yorker*. When the magazine said no, he crumpled up the letter, put away his pen, and went back to reading Civil War novels all weekend with his feet in the open oven for warmth. It worked: he never again had to feel the pain of having his work rejected by an editor.

Nor, incidentally, the joy of having it accepted. Which it probably would have been, eventually. There's scarcely a publication in the country that does not include essays by freelancers, from the *New York Times* to the op-ed pages of sleepy town newspapers. NPR broadcasts essays. Online magazines such as *Salon* and *Slate* fill page after page with them.

I've sold some essays over the years. I wrote about nagging for the "Everyday" section of Mervyns's California: It began, "In the morning my husband, Bill, stumbles into the kitchen after me and stares into the sink like a doomed man. 'Can I go on living with a woman who spits toothpaste in the kitchen sink?' he asks himself. 'Do I mention it, and rend the perfect harmonious fabric of our love, or stifle my rage anew every morning for the rest of my life?'"

I wrote about cheap men for the "Sexual Ethics" section of *Glamour* in which I included the story of a guy who asked if I wanted a drink after the movie and led me to a water fountain. When the new Beetles came out, I wrote an essay for *Via* magazine about the day I bought my own convertible Volkswagen after shuddering at sedans: "At the lot, as we looked at sedans in their neat rows, I felt my hair turn gray, my skin wrinkle, the dirt hit my casket." I wrote a piece in *Reader's Digest* about the long slow summers of my childhood. I wrote a piece for *MORE* magazine about the new grandmother, and one about how you start taking it easy on your mother in middle age. Send those essays out!

Of course you don't wanna. One student told me, "I'm not afraid of heights, or bears and rapists, but I'm scared to death of looking stupid, of having to give up my dreams, of having to realize that I can never be published in the *New York Times Magazine*." Then she adds, "And yet, when I pick up Oprah's *O* magazine, or I read an essay in *Real Simple*, or even the *New Yorker*, I think, I could have written that."

Hundreds of my students have published essays in newspapers and magazines, on radio, in columns. Rita Hargrave, a psychiatrist by day, publishes her pieces on salsa dancing in music magazines and writes about her work in trade publications. Stacey Appel writes a monthly essay for *Skirt!* magazine. Janis Cooke Newman has numerous articles and two books out, the second one a widely reviewed novel on Mary Todd Lincoln called *Mary*. Here are some of their emails to me about getting their work published:

```
It is so much fun to try to capture important moments
in words. I just love that! I get such a rush when
it's working, when I'm back to whatever moment it is
and slowing it down so I can dig into it and capture
it and translate it into words. And then I feel so
```

satisfied and touched when I can tell that it worked
for the readers. (**Evelyn Strauss**)

I sent [my essay] out and eight months later my phone
rings at 7 a.m. A woman on the other end sounds as if
she's hyperventilating and says she's an editor at
Cosmopolitan, has my manuscript, and wants to talk
about it. I say, "Knock it off, Mom. It's too early."
She convinces me who she is and says (I will never forget this), "We'll take it." (**Marsh Rose**)

I'd taken a First Person Writing workshop from you in
which you asked us to write five quirky (or odd) things
about ourselves. I wrote a piece that I titled "My Big
Fat Greek Hair" from that assignment. And one afternoon,
in a moment of bravado and having had a large Peet's
coffee, I called the articles editor at *O*. Her outgoing message said something like, "We do not work with
freelancers. We do not take unsolicited pitches. Do not
leave a message. Do not send a manuscript." Basically,
go away. I left a message anyway, giving her the title
of my piece. She called back thirty seconds later and
asked me to email it to her. While they didn't take that
essay, they took another piece. (**Christina Boufis**)

They love it, it's just what they wanted, and since
they are editing it down to a running length of
2,000 words they are going to pay me *only* $3,000.
THREE THOUSAND DOLLARS!!! Excuse me, I have to go
faint. (**Holly Rose**)

My student Jessa Vartanian, a thirty-year-old high-tech writer living in San Jose, California, became one of several revolving columnists in the "Our So-Called Lives" section in the Sunday living section
of the *San Jose Mercury News*. She made it happen. She put together

samples and a cover letter and sent them in, but then heard nothing for three months. The editor finally called to say she was leaving the paper and was passing Jessa's stuff on to the features editor, named Holly.

"Two or three months later," Jessa said, "Holly called me out of the blue to say she wanted to run a piece. After that I kept sending her stuff. I figured you make a contact, you keep your face in front of them. I kept saying, by the way, I'd love to be a regular contributor. She called a month later, and then again, to accept pieces, then called one day to say she wanted me to contribute on a regular basis."

Jessa did it for two and a half years, receiving $75 a column and writing mostly about dating. "It's the exposure that matters, not the money," she said. "I open my guts and say what's going on in my life. I think everyone has the same basic thoughts but people don't say them out loud, so it's comforting when people can relate to the same experiences I've had. That's very satisfying."

If you write a good piece, and keep sending it out, sooner or later it will be published. There's a vast hungry maw out there that needs your work, legions of editors who are paid to read your submissions and put them in print. Few writers take gladly to this step in the process—selling—but once you start doing it and start getting pieces accepted, it won't seem so daunting. You will establish a list of editors who like and look forward to your work, and you won't have to slap the bushes to see what flies up.

Where to Find a Market

Dedicate a day or two to familiarizing yourself with the many outlets for personal essays. *Writer's Market* has a yearly compendium both in print and online, and how-to magazines for writers, such as *Writer's Digest*, regularly feature lists of publications to write for. You will mainly be looking at newspapers, magazines, the Internet, and, increasingly, public radio.

Once you have identified some publications you might want to approach, type "submissions [name of publication]" into your search engine and see what pops up. (I should caution you that the search results for *essays* tend to give you a list of people eager to write a paper on Robert Frost for you for a fee.) Keep in mind that the information below, like anything in print—and especially anything related to publishing—may need updating by the time you read it.

NEWSPAPERS

Newspapers are a good bet for first-person essays. They publish far more of them than they used to. These days you can find first-person essays on feature pages, on op-ed pages (opposite the editorial page), and in special sections. Start out by sending pieces to local publications, not overlooking the free ones, the neighborhood shopping guides, anything. Neighborhood papers use essays, too, and often feature them nicely on a page by themselves. The *Noe Valley Voice* in San Francisco, for example, has a "Last Page" section that runs essays by local freelancers.

MAGAZINES

Many, many magazines publish personal essays. I pick up issues in doctors' offices and flip to the back page, where I usually find a standing feature called "Last [something]." These pieces are often light, well-constructed, and fun to read. Here are some examples: Steven Lewis writes in the "Last Word" of the *Ladies' Home Journal*, "The world can be divided into those who will let a telephone ring off the hook when they are even mildly indisposed and those who would cheerfully trample small children and flower beds rather than let it hit the third ring." Carrie St. Michel writes in *Good Housekeeping*'s "Light Housekeeping" section about her eight-year-old son's obsession with moussing his hair. Constance Resemble writes in the *New York Times* travel section about how she wished she were a more intrepid traveler, but she really liked seeing places from little trains.

The catch is that while newspapers are aimed at everybody, each magazine's demographics are different. The majority of *Ladies' Home Journal* readers are thirty-eight to forty-two years old. *MORE* magazine targets women over forty. The *Redbook* reader is college-educated, married, and anywhere from her late twenties to early forties. *Cosmopolitan* is aimed at college students. I sold about twenty-four pieces to its now-defunct "On My Mind" section (I called my husband, Bill, my "boyfriend," which I hope is still part of his job description).

I know you blanched at that list of familiar supermarket titles—you don't read them, and so you can't imagine writing for them. Don't be fooled. Magazines are great outlets, and those simple little essays are not so simple to publish. Long before an essay hits the supermarket shelves, the writer had to get to know the magazine, what it had published before, who the readers were, and what the editors were looking for. The best way to determine the audience (demographic) for a magazine is to look at the ads. Advertisers don't throw their money around—they know exactly who buys the magazine. If you flip through the pages and don't see advertisements for diapers, send your piece on hiring that under-caffeinated princess for your two-year-old's party elsewhere.

Here's a sampling of magazines that publish personal essays (remember, this information may need updating):

Send your piece on how your dog helped you overcome an obstacle to *Dog Fancy* magazine. *The Bark*, which also covers canine culture, uses at least a couple of essays in each issue. Past examples include a woman who researched the language of dogs after she noticed her own puppy "laughing," and a woman who sees dogs in a new light through the eyes of her children. They're looking for 1,200 to 1,500 words.

One of the best (and probably hardest to get into) outlets is the "Lives" column in the Sunday *New York Times Magazine*. They're looking for provocative and fresh viewpoints (the maximum length is 900 words). They also publish the "Modern Love" feature in that paper's Sunday style section.

Check out the "Life Lessons" feature in *Real Simple* magazine.

Redbook runs first-person essays about dramatic or pivotal moments in a woman's life.

Newsweek publishes an essay a week in its "My Turn" section.

Fine Gardening features humorous personal essays in "Last Word." A recent essay talked about people who label their plants.

Brain, Child is a literary magazine dedicated "to the meatier issues of motherhood." In a recent piece, a white mother discussed styling the hair of her adopted African-American baby.

Plenty magazine looks for witty personal essays of about 750 words that explore a humorous or moving experience in the realm of "going green." Past essays include a mother who gave up her gas-guzzling car to become a pedestrian and a woman who owns an eco-friendly home in the mountains. *OnEarth* magazine publishes personal essays on nature or the environment.

The Sun runs a number of literary essays, some of them pretty long. Past examples include a story about a woman in a relationship with an abusive drug addict and a story of a Fulbright scholar who comes to terms with her prosthetic leg while living with a troubled host family in South Korea.

Creative Non-Fiction has themed issues. They feature the best new creative nonfiction writers and are open to personal essays. Guidelines and upcoming themes are posted on their website.

Backpacker features a regular "Backcountry" section that runs 1,200-word personal essays about lessons learned while backpacking.

Bereavement: A Magazine of Hope and Healing, a magazine for people dealing with grief, looks for personal experience pieces of 2,000 words or less. It doesn't pay but offers writers international exposure.

Cup of Comfort, the best-selling anthology series, features creative nonfiction stories and narrative essays about experiences and relationships that comfort, inspire, and enrich.

Field and Stream has a regular "Finally" section that runs an essay of 700 to 800 words every month.

Smithsonian Magazine prints essays on the "Last Page" that range from 550 to 700 words and usually have a humorous tone. The editors warn, however, that they want personal narrative, not jokes.

It's smart to check out corporate magazines, too. There are thousands of these custom magazines, such as *Safeway Select*. They lack the glory of *Vanity Fair*, admittedly, but they pay well and are much easier to break into.

Airline magazines love little insider destination pieces. (Just make sure the place you write about is on their route.) I did pieces on San Francisco's microclimates and the sea lions that live at Pier 39 for American Airlines' *American Way* magazine. One of my students sold them a piece about Jelly's, a salsa place on the San Francisco waterfront that is so cool that people take cabs there directly from the airport.

THE INTERNET

When you publish in cyberspace, the rules change. Depending on the site, you can write to any length, use swear words, email it in. Many of my students have published work in *Skirt!* magazine, which appears both in print and online. One issue alone ran sixteen personal essays, among them one about depression, one about spring (the season of being dragged to weddings by soon-to-be ex-girlfriends), and one by a married woman who likes to sleep alone.

After your piece appears on the Web, you can print it out, and it will look like any other clip (or attach the URL to your outgoing email so everyone can enjoy it). A *clip* is a copy of a piece that has appeared in print; writers who propose a piece to a magazine editor will often enclose clips to show the editor what their writing is like. Or, these days, often a writer might just direct an editor to URLs where her work can be read.

Salon (www.salon.com), which publishes smart and topical personal essays, offers advice for contributors that is typical of many online publications:

```
We ask that you please send the text of your query or
submission in plain text in the body of your email,
rather than as an attached file, as we may not be able
to read the format of your file.

    If you wish to contribute, please spend some time
familiarizing yourself with Salon's various sections and
regular features. Please put the words "EDITORIAL SUB-
MISSIONS" in the subject line of the email. You can find
the editor's name on our Salon Staff page. And please
```

tell us a little about yourself—your experience and background as a writer and qualifications for writing a particular story. If you have clips you can send us via email, or Web addresses of pages that contain your work, please send us a representative sampling (no more than three or four, please). Unless your pitch relates to breaking news, please send your submission during business hours.

We do our best to respond to all inquiries, but be aware that we are sometimes inundated. If you have not heard back from us after three weeks, please assume that we will not be able to use your idea or submission.

RADIO

Many of my students have read their short (two-minute) essays (300 to 375 words) on topics of local interest over the radio on Perspective on KQED, the San Francisco Bay Area's local NPR station (www.kqed.org/radio/perspectives/submissions.html). Other NPR stations offer this, too.

NPR's *This I Believe* seeks personal essays. Be sure to read the essay-writing tips on their site (http://thisibelieve.org/guidelines).

How to Find Hooks

Whether you're submitting to a local paper, a national monthly magazine, or an Internet site, you want to offer them a reason to publish your piece in this particular publication at this particular time. These are called *hooks*. (*Hook*, confusingly enough, is also a term meaning to hook the reader into reading a piece.)

LOCAL

Local publications want local pieces by local writers. Stay alert for ways to tie what you have written to something happening near you. If developers are tearing down historic houses to build a mall and you once lived in one of them, bingo.

You can also send your piece to the region where it happened. One student's piece about a fellow worker killed in a volcano in Hawaii was published in the op-ed page of the *Honolulu Star*. Refer to the local place in the piece: "At Yoshi's the other night . . ." or "I was walking on one of the Mount Diablo trails . . ."

TOPICAL

Relate your piece to something that is happening in the news. If you once dated Prince Charles and he's coming to town, that's an angle for a piece on princes, on dating, or on your sorry relationship history. The governor of South Carolina is walking the Appalachian Trail? You hiked it once yourself. If you used a Wilson tennis racquet to become junior league tennis champion when you were twelve, and Wilson is going out of business, there's an angle for a nostalgic piece. If the news is full of Olympic ice skaters, hit editors with your piece on taking up ice skating at the age of forty-one.

My student Rita Hargrave used a topical hook when she sent this note to the *St. Louis Post-Dispatch* in November of 2008 and got an acceptance by return email.

> The toughest domestic challenge for President-elect Obama and First Lady Michelle when they step into the White House won't be housebreaking the First Puppy or choosing a china pattern. The real battleground will be what to do with Malia and Sasha's fuzzy locks. Press or perm? Afro-puffs or pageboy? It's the age-old struggle between African-American mothers and daughters. I hope the enclosed essay, "The Trouble with My Hair," will interest the readers of your newspaper.

My student Margee Robinson, who lives in San Francisco, sold a piece on earthquake preparedness to the *San Francisco Chronicle*, sending it in just before the 100th anniversary of the 1906 quake in San Francisco. The hook was twofold: topical and local.

> **try this**
> Read the paper and find five hot topics that you can connect to your essays. If you come across an issue that you can relate to but haven't written about yet, jot it down for future inspiration.

SEASONAL

Seasonal topics are almost as good as topical ones. Valentine's Day is a good bet for your piece on matchmaking or your third-grade love, the one who bought you a stupid bottle of cologne encased in a pink plastic swan. If you're writing about a family dinner, why not make it Thanksgiving? Publish your piece about your mother's breast cancer in October, which is Breast Cancer Awareness Month. My student Pat Milton published "Stalking the Winter Coat" in April. That's late for winter coats, but she fixed that by noting that she bought the coat in an end-of-season sale. You can get calendars that list all sorts of obscure events, such as National Salmon Fishermen's Week.

Have a piece about volunteering in school? Send it out in time for it to appear in late August, when school starts up. (Magazines plan six months ahead of time, so keep that in mind). My student Karen wrote her father into a piece about spare change and it was accepted for Father's Day.

Magazines and certain sections of newspapers have editorial calendars that list special theme issues ahead of time. The *New York Times Magazine*, for example, sets aside specific weeks for subjects such as men and health, cars, giving, travel, home design, and so on.

A Word About Rights

Let's get the discussion of rights out of the way. A *copyright* is legal ownership of a written work. You need do nothing to obtain it: You own the copyright automatically the minute you produce the work. (In 1978, the law was changed to say you own it for your lifetime plus seventy years.) Don't put a big fat © for copyright on your pages—it'll just scream amateur.

Rights vary from publication to publication, both those in print and online. In general, when you sell your work to a publication, you are not selling the manuscript itself but the right to publish it, under stated terms. When the publication buys *first serial rights*, they are buying the right to publish the piece first. Once they have published it, you own the right to publish it again. (Some contracts state that this right reverts to you in sixty days.) Be careful about giving away all rights to a publication—it means they own your work forever.

Newspapers buy one-time rights in their own geographic area. This means you can sell the same piece at the same time to other papers outside their publishing zone. If you're selling your essay to the *San Francisco Chronicle*, you can also send it to the *Seattle Times*, the *Boston Globe*, and the *Miami Herald*—but not to, say, the *San Jose Mercury News*, based an hour south, which would compete.

If you are on staff for a publication, as I was at the *Chronicle*, they own the rights to your work. However, you can ask them to return the rights to you later, as I did with my columns.

How to Submit

Submitting your essay isn't nearly as easy as it may seem—it involves much more than hitting "send" or printing out your essay, stuffing it into an envelope, and dropping it in a mailbox. Here are some techniques and strategies to present your work in the best possible light.

STICK TO THE WORD COUNT

If you're submitting something to a publication that runs 800-word essays, don't send them a 1,000-word piece with the idea that the editors will either alter their format to accommodate your wonderful piece or will cut it down to 800 words themselves. Also, make sure it doesn't resemble something they just ran. Their publication is their baby, and they like to think you read it.

SEND ONE PIECE AT A TIME

Although it may be tempting to send an editor your entire writing portfolio since high school (there's bound to be one in here they like, right?), refrain from doing so. Pick your strongest piece and start there.

KNOW WHEN AND HOW TO SEND IT

You can email or fax your piece if it's "time-bound"—for instance, it's a Father's Day piece and has to run in June or not at all. Otherwise, find out whether the publication prefers mailed or emailed submissions. (Forget those rush delivery services—you should see the piles of unopened FedEx packages marked "URGENT! Open immediately!" tossed to the back of cubicles along with the promo toys and press releases. Save your money.)

Emailing submissions is becoming more and more the standard, and many publications have switched to an online submission process. In your email, put the section you're submitting to in the subject line: "Real Lives."

MULTIPLE SUBMISSIONS: PROCEED WITH CAUTION

Can you submit the same piece to different publications at the same time? (This is called making "multiple submissions.") It's not a problem to do that with newspapers, generally, but magazines might not look at your piece if they know you're sending it to others at the same time. So it's your decision whether to increase your chances by doing that, and whether to let the editor know. My only hint is to say that you get caught only when you have multiple acceptances, which may be a problem you wish to have.

KEEP TRACK OF SUBMISSIONS

Keep a list of your submissions by date, article, and publication. This makes it easier when you want to call an editor and say, "I sent you a piece on such-and-such a date."

KNOW WHEN TO QUERY

A *query* is a proposal to write a piece. Professional magazine writers query a piece before writing it; that is, they describe the article and get a contract to write it, tailoring it specifically for the publication.

Humor and first-person pieces are rarely sold with queries, because so much of an essay's appeal lies in charm rather than content. The editor has to read the whole thing to know if he wants it. Imagine E. B. White trying to sell what became a famous essay this way: "Here are three thousand words on my pig. Would you like to buy it?" Or an unknown Joan Didion pitching a piece on headaches: "I get migraines a lot, and I have written an essay about this experience. Would you like to read it?"

INCLUDE A COVER NOTE

Provide a brief description of the piece and how it relates to the publication's needs. Explain why you are telling this particular story at this particular time and why people will want to read it. List any relevant publishing credits you have. (If you haven't been published before, don't bring up the subject of clips.)

Try to spark their interest. Editors sometimes know from a one-line description in the cover letter whether they're going to want the piece or not. One editor said when he read the line, "Enclosed, please find my essay about how I fell in love with the nurse while getting a colonoscopy," he just knew, before he even read it, that he had to buy that piece. On the other hand, lines like "Enclosed, please find my piece about life and love and redemption" can have the opposite effect.

DROP NAMES IF YOU HAVE NAMES TO DROP

Here's a cover note my student Nancy Devine emailed to a magazine that subsequently accepted her essay:

> Laurie Kretchmar, a writer, editor, and former editor
> of *Working Woman*, asked me to send you this essay. She

said she liked how I described the way time expanded or contracted for me as a mother. I am a health writer who also loves writing essays. I have written for *Nurse-Week*, *HealthWeek*, *Eternelle*, *WebRN*, and several Stanford University newsletters, among other publications.

If you know a writer or pretty much anybody who works at the publication, ask that person if you can say something like, "I'm writing at the suggestion of so-and-so."

SWEAT THE SMALL STUFF

Double-space your piece, leaving wide margins. If you're emailing, many editors prefer that you just copy your submission into the email itself, to spare them the risk and bother of clicking on an attachment (which may have viruses).

Proofread carefully to see if you any words out. (Ha!) If the presentation of your work matters to the person who's going to buy your manuscript, it matters to you. I'm not the most meticulous person in the world, but I see the logic: how will your editor know you can do the hard thing—make an essay compelling, lively, and meaningful—if you can't do the easy thing and catch those typos, blank pages, and coffee stains?

Go to the publication's website and find the name of the editor in charge of the section. If the email addresses of the editors aren't listed, go to the advertising/sales section to see how the company's email addresses are formatted—the editors' will be formatted the same way. In your correspondence, get the editor's title right and spell her name right. (When I was an editor at *San Francisco Focus* magazine I once got a letter addressed to "Adair Lard.")

GET AN ANSWER

If you are sending only the manuscript and you don't want it back, just enclose a stamped, self-addressed postcard with your return address on the front. On the back type the following, adding boxes:

```
NAME OF ARTICLE:
I can use this, will advise when. ❑
I may be able to use this, will hold. ❑
I can't use this. ❑
COMMENTS:
NAME AND PUBLICATION:
```

Give the publication some time before following up with an email. After a few weeks have passed, send an email along the lines of:

```
I sent you a piece entitled "[title]" on [date] and want-
ed to check to see if you've had a chance to look it
over. I hope to hear from you soon.
```

If you've submitted your piece and sent a follow-up email but still have heard nothing back, can you call them? Yes, but wait as long as possible. Freelance submissions are submissions nobody asked to see. The editor needs them, but first she has to hustle upstairs and find out why the four spreads she was promised for Saturday were cut to two, and edit the piece on 1950s drive-ins that just came in, and wade through her email. Also, your piece is probably buried under her lunch and the ton of magazines, mail, and cardboard flats of plants that have also been sent in unsolicited. You might try calling after or before hours, so she can get your message and hunt down the piece before she calls you back.

How to Handle Rejections

You can't decide you're going to be published. You have no control over what the editors out there do. But you can follow F. Scott Fitzgerald's example and decide to paper the room in rejection slips before you get discouraged. Rejection slips prove you're a working writer. (Plus they're useful to show the IRS when you deduct the expenses of your freelance business, including a home office, travel, and lunches, so make copies or photograph your wall.)

A rejection with a handwritten note on it that says, "We can't use this, but try us again," is *very* good. Editors write such messages only to writers they want to encourage. They know you'll be so excited at their interest that you'll back a van up to their back door and dump in everything you've ever written. For instance, my student Carol Lena got this letter for a short story she sent out:

```
Thank you for sending us "Physics of Love." Unfortu-
nately this particular work was not a right fit for our
publication, but I was very impressed by your writing.
There is much to admire in your selection of detail,
development of character, and clean, confident prose.
This piece may benefit from greater attention to scene
in its early pages; scenes in the present action,
rather than backstory, might help develop tension and
reader engagement early. Please remember that this is
the opinion of only one reader. Thank you for trying
us, and we look forward to reading more.
```

Rejection notes, either nice personal ones like this or terse "Sorry, we can't use this," are part of the writing process. Most magazines publish less than 2 percent of what floods into their white plastic U.S. Mailboxes every morning. Be persistent. If your work has energy, and you can spell, it is virtually guaranteed that you will be published sooner or later. My student Kathleen Denny, for example, emailed me to say that a local paper had published a piece she'd done a couple of years before about the work-summer vacation tension, from the vantage point of an airline mechanic. Kathleen wrote, "A couple years ago, no one was interested, but this editor loved it. Persistence pays off!"

Kim Ratclif emailed me to say, "I wrote a piece in your class and sent it to *Garden Design*'s "Dirt" section. Never heard a peep out of them until two and a half years later. New editor finds it at the bottom of his slush pile, likes it, has me update it, and runs it!"

And remember, if an editor takes the time for a personal rejection, thank him for that—it takes extra effort on his part and it might help him remember you the next time you submit something.

How to Handle Acceptances

Be professionally friendly with editors. Thank them for running your piece—the featured-space layout, the stunning artwork, the light touch with editing. Be, uh, submissive. Don't argue over how the piece was edited, don't go over their heads when they never get back to you at all. Just move on. Pay no attention at first to whether you are paid or how much—that all comes later. Big-city newspapers tend to pay only $75 to $150 for freelance essays, while national magazines pay well—I received $5,000 for a 2,000-word piece on being a grandma from *MORE* magazine.

BEING EDITED

How much you let editors mess with your writing is likely to depend on where you are in your writing career and how personal the piece is. I myself let magazines do whatever they like—I even let *MORE* magazine run the essay above that made it sound as if I didn't like my grandkids. (When it came out, I answered emails from indignant grannies accusing me of being hard hearted, and could hardly type my replies because I was holding two-year-old Maggie and four-year-old Ryan in my lap.)

It's fairly common for a new writer to be so distressed at what "they" did to the piece that she asks to have the byline removed. Resist the impulse to do this, unless the piece is so personal and close to your heart that you can't allow it to go into print with the changes. Editors work hard, most of them improve a piece, and it just doesn't pay to complain. Enjoy your check and go on to the next piece.

Get Your Work Out There

I urge you to submit your work for publication. Start by sending something to some faraway newspaper or magazine, just to say you did it. My students have published thousands of essays over the years. In fact, most get published within a year of taking a class. Not all of them do, though. Only the ones who send work out.

In the next chapter, we move on from publishing essays to publishing the full-length memoir, so this is a good place to mention that if you're interested in getting a memoir published, you might start by sending some excerpts to magazines. Those excerpts will impress your future editor and might even land that editor: You can go to an agent or editor and say, "Here's a piece that was published in the *New York Times*. I'm working on a memoir about it." Author Sue Shapiro remarked that the magazine pieces she published about smoking gave momentum to her memoir, *Lighting Up*. Another incentive to get your shorter pieces in circulation is that editors and agents troll through magazines in search of promising writers to talk into doing a book.

One more thing: Once you have a number of autobiographical essays compiled, whether they have been published or not, it might be possible to link them together to form a book. Consider *The Boys of My Youth* by Jo Ann Beard. It's billed as a collection of stories, but the recurring character is named Jo Ann and the family members are the same from essay to essay. Is it a memoir or a collection of discrete essays? Hard to say. Another example is *Family Bible* by Melissa J. Delbridge, a collection of personal essays about growing up in Tuscaloosa.

Or, moving on to the next chapter, you can write a memoir and get it published. Many, many people have successfully shepherded their opus from the kitchen table to a proud place on bookstore shelves. The next chapter will tell you how they did it.

fourteen

PUBLISHING YOUR MEMOIR

If there's a book you really want to read,
but it hasn't been written yet, then you must write it.

—TONI MORRISON

SUDDENLY IN the 1990s, everybody was writing and publishing and reading memoirs. That trend hasn't slowed down: It's easier to publish a memoir these days than a novel. You don't have to be famous first anymore—you can be famous afterward.

The very popularity of memoir, however, means you have to work harder to make the one you write different from what's already out there. There are lots of memoirs now on various subjects: for example, illness (Lori Gottlieb's *Stick Figure: A Diary of My Former Self*) and drinking (Caroline Knapp's *Drinking: A Love Story*). There are lots of memoirs set in mental wards, such as Susanna Kaysen's *Girl, Interrupted*. One of my students, working on a book about her stroke, found a dozen or more memoirs already out on the subject. That doesn't mean she can't do hers—it just means she has to find a new angle—or *premise*, as it's called when you're talking about a book.

As I've mentioned (somewhat piteously) earlier, I've been working for about 150 years on a memoir of my childhood. Talk about memoirs that have already been done! Books on bad childhoods include the titles that helped launch the memoir craze, such as Tobias Wolff's *This*

Boy's Life, Jeannette Walls's *The Glass Castle*, Mary Karr's *The Liars' Club*, and Frank McCourt's *Angela's Ashes*. Way worse fathers than mine! To get my memoir published, it will have to cover new ground or I will have to write the hell out of it, or probably both.

On the other hand, nobody knows what will succeed and what will flop. Write the craziest book you can imagine, if you want to. That's my plan, anyway. But don't do the craziest thing you can imagine to bring it to the attention of the publishing marketplace: follow the procedures set up by those gatekeepers to your dreams, the literary agents and the acquisitions editors at publishing houses.

Find an Agent

The days of sending a book straight to a publisher are gone, unless you are targeting a university press or a small press. You will need an agent. This book was sold for me by my agent, Kitty Cowles, who liked Ten Speed's list of writing books and thought mine might be a good fit.

An agent is someone who agrees to represent your book in all dealings with a publisher. The agent decides which editors at which publishing houses would be interested in it and sends it to a select number of them. When the book is accepted, the agent gets you the best deal possible and tracks the book thereafter, helping sell foreign rights or paperback rights, and troubleshooting (including, if necessary, turning the editor upside down until your check falls out of his pockets). For these services, the agent usually gets 15 percent of your royalties. He or she will earn that percentage: agents are wily.

Susan Parker, author of *Tumbling After*, about taking care of her quadriplegic husband, told me her first agent dropped her after the editors who'd seen it complained that the book was "too dark, not enough about Ralph, not enough reflection." Though the book was done, her new agent, Amy Rennert, sent out just fifty pages—the least dark, the most reflective, and the most about Susan's husband, Ralph, who had been paralyzed in a biking accident. It sold.

My former agent, Fred Hill, got *Hold Me Close* into a New York auction. (That's when several publishing houses bid on the same day.)

Random House (actually its subdivision Broadway Books), the winner (and the only bidder, due to some confusion, but never mind), gave me an advance of $110,000 for it, which I promptly put into about-to-crash tech stocks, while a writer friend shrewdly put his advance into a twelfth-century Tuscan villa that he still owns (but never mind that either).

A good way to find an agent, besides asking around, is to go to a large bookstore and leaf through books that are like yours. Note which agents are thanked in the acknowledgments, then contact them. (Dave Eggers has said he sought out David Sedaris's agent, for example.) LiteraryAgents.com is a good place to find names, too. You might pony up for Publishers Lunch, an insider newsletter that tells which agents are doing the hot deals. (Find it at www.publishersmarketplace.com.)

Take your time on this part of the process: You don't want to spend years of your precious hours on earth writing and polishing all those pages and only five minutes on the question of who is going to shepherd your baby into the world for you. (Avoid agents who charge a reading fee, by the way.)

If you can drop a name, do it. Contacts are as useful in publishing as they are in any other business. It's easier to sell work to agents or editors you know personally. Susan Parker said that of the thirteen houses her first agent sent *Tumbling After* to, only the editor at Norton whom Susan had met at a workshop, showed interest. (It was ulti-mately sold to Crown.)

A lot of the agents and editors live in New York, of course, and you may not want to move there on the off chance of smacking into one of them while jogging in Central Park. But writing workshops and con-ferences are held all over the country, and they offer a chance to find yourself reaching for the buffet shrimp alongside agents, editors, and famous authors. There's a list of these conferences in every issue of *Poets & Writers* magazine. Do editors or agents offer workshops near you? Sign up for them. When you're ready, send them an email that says, "I met you at the Squaw Valley Community of Writers, and . . ."

Prepare to Obsess Over the Query Letter

Once you have gathered the names of agents you want to approach, what's the next step? You don't send them the book. You don't even send them the entire book proposal. (I know we haven't talked about book proposals yet, but believe me, we will.) You send them a *query*, in which you try to convince them you are a hot writer with a hot project. You want to have your book proposal ready to go when you send out these queries, so you can send it to whoever asks to see it.

The query is one page—no more than 300 words. You'll sweat over it more than any other page you write. An agent is not going to sign up the writer of a boring query letter. Agent Elizabeth Evans said at a conference I attended, "If the first paragraph is pedestrian in its language I won't read further." If the first paragraph of your book is fabulous, you can make that the first paragraph of your query. Mention the arc—how you change over the course of the tale you tell.

Put a simple header at the top of the page giving your name, address, telephone number, and email address. Present your query double-spaced, on plain white paper, with 12-point type in a black font (Times New Roman is good). If you're emailing, write "Query: [title of book]" in the subject line. If snail-mailing, include a self-addressed stamped envelope for replies. Use block paragraphs—no indentations.

Don't begin "Dear Sir." Big turnoff. And the whole "Mr." business is going by the way. Use the agent's whole name—"Dear Jack Lawson." Show Jack Lawson you didn't just cut and paste his name in from a list on Internet. "I am writing to you because you represented *I Was a Teenaged Professor* and I think my book, *I Was a Preschool English Department Chairman*, is similar." Be respectful. Agent Kimberly Cameron got a query that began, "Hey, Knucklehead! How much jingle can you get me?"

Then give us a single sentence that says what's in the book. Sue Shapiro said she pitched *Five Men Who Broke My Heart* by saying in the query, "Here's a memoir for anyone who's ever wondered what happened to their first love, or second, or third, or fourth, or fifth."

The agent knows there are no truly fresh ideas, only fresh spins on old ones. Tell him your spin. Pretend you're on a talk show and have less than a minute to get your book across. (I was on book tour in Louisville, Kentucky, with Morgan, heading sleepily to some predawn farm TV program, when our guide said, "Think sound bites! You won't have much time!") The agent has a lot to do and wants to put your letter in the "No Thanks" pile and go on to the next. Your job is to get him to pick up his Blackberry instead.

In its traditional form, a query letter has three concise paragraphs: the hook, the minisynopsis, and your writer's biography. The website QueryTracker.net has a terrific section on this, with specific examples. In the letter, stick to the manuscript—no need to talk about how you will market the book, and for goodness sake don't mention other books you have waiting in the pipeline after he's looked at this one.

The next paragraph gives the agent your credentials. Say something about your background, why you wrote the book. Do you have an MFA? Are you an experienced published writer? Appeared in literary magazines? (I've heard that moves you to the top of the pile.)

If you've never been published before, no reason to bring that up now is there? You do, by the way, have an advantage in having no sales figure track record: You have never failed. Your book could be the next *Eat, Pray, Love.* Experienced authors with fifteen titles (books that did all right but did not "break out," as they say) change their names so they can burst on the scene with all the freshness of a pretty girl at her first dance.

Keep the tone of the letter quiet and assured. In other words, don't sell the book. That's the agent's job. Don't give her the hype; just the facts (the persuasive facts, of course). Let her discover you.

Write the query out long and then punch it down to one page. Hone it. Make it exciting and interesting, and concise. End by saying, "I would love to send you my proposal."

Here are a few things you shouldn't say (as my father said, don't supply the rocks that are to be thrown at you):

    I'm an unpublished writer.

```
I don't know if this will interest you.
I had a bad experience with another publisher.
```

Some agents prefer queries to come in the regular mail with a self-addressed, stamped envelope. Others like email. Check their websites to find out whether they have a preference. Yes, you can send the query to several agents at once, but it's considered fair to let them know you're doing it. Then be patient. They're busy.

Don't be discouraged that you don't land an agent on your first or second round of inquiries; it can take time. Interested agents will often respond by asking you to send partial pages or the whole manuscript or your book proposal (more on this in the next section).

Once one or more agents show interest, by the way, it might be your turn to be choosy. Find someone who has successfully sold projects, of course, but also someone who seems to like and understand your book, in addition to being convinced she can sell it. He may or may not ask you to sign a contract. Some agents will ask you to redo the proposal or make editing suggestions on the book; some won't.

Put Together the Proposal

A proposal outlines what you're going to do in the book, how it's different from everything else out there, why you're the best person to write it, and who will buy it. Here's what to include.

AN EYE-CATCHING TITLE

You'll need a good title, even if the editor changes it later. My first agent hated the title of this book. He said there's nothing inside about being naked or drunk (which is true, as I cut the part about how Victor Hugo and Benjamin Franklin wrote naked). But I thought it would get the book more attention than the other titles I fiddled with, such as *Turning Your Worst Moments into Money* or *Dance Lessons*. Besides, you have the subtitle in a memoir to say exactly what the book is about.

I had a hard time choosing a title for my memoir about my daughter. (A friend, Mark Sloan, suggested I call it *Chicken Soup for What's*

Left of Your Soul After Your Teenager Has Ripped Your Heart Out of Your Chest and Stomped on It with Her Platform Sneakers.)

Titles and covers are marketing devices, and thus the publisher's call. My friend Janis Cooke Newman wanted to call her novel about Mary Todd Lincoln *The Madhouse Summer of Mary Todd Lincoln*, which I thought was a fabulous title, but the publisher wanted titles such as *Asylum*, and they finally compromised on *Mary*. I wanted to call my book on being a grandmother *Know When to Hold 'Em: Playing Your Cards Right as a New Grandmother*, but the sales and marketing folks at Chronicle Books didn't go for it, and they're the ones who have to get the thing into the bookstores. It's called *The Granny Diaries*, to coast off the success of *The Nanny Diaries*.

A BRIEF OVERVIEW

The overview should summarize what your book is about in one or two pages. If who you are and the work you do is a selling point, these go into the overview. Include the timeliness of the topic: Is it something that's in the news a lot lately? Did *Newsweek* do a cover story on the topic you're writing about? Include a copy. Say why you decided to write the book, what you think its key lessons are, who you think is the audience.

A COMPELLING BIO

Include pertinent information about yourself. Don't be modest. Who are you? What makes you an expert on this subject? Most importantly, what gives you a platform? A *platform* is a way to reach the audience. Do you give workshops? Presentations? Have a website that gets lots of hits? Have you been featured in national magazines, on TV or radio? Most of us will not have impressive answers, but don't worry. Neither did many now-famous authors when they started out. Skip that part of your achievements that have nothing to do with the book or its subject.

By the way, don't waste a lot of time talking about what you will do to promote the book. Mention instead *what you are already doing*. Everyone can make their book a best seller if they get on Oprah, but don't even bother mentioning this unless you've been on Oprah before or the two of you play tennis on Sundays. Say you have five hundred friends on Facebook, that you speak at the Rotary Club, that twenty friends will throw you a book party (at which your book will be sold, natch).

ANY MEDIA MATERIAL

Include anything that says what a star you are. Supply your agent with newspaper and magazine clips, tapes of radio and TV performances, copies of articles you've written or been interviewed for. It's better to send too much rather than too little. Your agent can weed through it and decide what's useful. Are you cute? Do you have an author photo? It can't hurt to include it.

A MARKET ANALYSIS

Create a marketing overview that says who will want to buy this book. Come up with numbers if you can: If your book will appeal to those who adopt Chinese orphans, tell your prospective agent and editor how many such families there are. Publishers aren't impressed when you airily claim your book appeals to "Oh, everyone." They want to know what shelf the bookstore will put it on (and which talk shows will be interested).

HOW IT DIFFERS FROM THE COMPETITION

Are there similar books out there? Show how your book stands out from them. Imagine your book on that shelf in the bookstore with other books on bulimia. How is your approach different? Name the top three or so competitive books and be specific about how yours is way different (and way better). Maybe your memoir on breast cancer specifically focuses on women of color, or how it affects one's kids. (By the way, *read* those other books.) You can start your search on Amazon.com, which is the first place the agent and editor will go to look up books like yours. And it's never a bad idea to spend an afternoon in a big bookstore, looking over titles.

A TABLE OF CONTENTS AND CHAPTER SUMMARIES

Include a nicely formatted table of contents and chapter summaries—short chapter-by-chapter breakdowns of the entire book. This is the editor's first real look at the way you write, so work on them and make them fun to read—that is, don't start each one by droning, "Chapter One will include . . ." Put your voice into it and make them read as if they were the chapters themselves.

SAMPLE CHAPTERS

The proposal will include two to three sample chapters or two chapters and an introduction, though sometimes you can also get away with just emailing the first twenty-five terrific pages, depending on the agent's preferences. When choosing which sample chapters to include, don't just automatically go to the first. What chapters are your strongest and most intriguing?

The grammar, punctuation, and style should be perfect. This is annoying to me, because you haven't written the whole book yet, and you know I stress not polishing anything until the whole piece of writing is at least roughly in place. You would think an editor could overloook a few tyops or **strange** fonts . . .

ENDORSEMENTS

It's not a bad idea to include blurbs in the proposal. A blurb is a short sales pitch or comment on a book that's used on the jacket or in marketing materials. Get your famous friend to give you a blurb you can use right in the pitch letter. Blurbs from the famous work best, of course, but exuberant testimonials even from unknowns can work, too. Sometimes busy people will say yes if you offer to write the blurb for them: "I need something like this . . ."

OTHER INFO

Make sure your proposal has page numbers. And say how long the book will be and how long it will take you, once the book is under contract, to deliver your complete manuscript.

All of this information, and a lot more, is on the Web. There are also people—I'm not one of them—who specialize in helping writers with their book proposals.

Of course, editors will have a wide variety of responses to your book. When my agent sent out the manuscript of *Hold Me Close*, an editor at Morrow wanted more "inner emotional landscape." Another editor at a different house wanted the book to be "more edgy, more emotional and more introspective." Then an editor from Scribner called me. "I like this book because it doesn't wallow," she said.

When the agent sells the book, you have a new person in your life: your editor. The editor may want further revisions. Be advised—new authors are said to be the most demanding and the most resistant to revision. Be cool. Don't pester. Don't demand to know the marketing plan right away, don't refer to the treatment other authors get, and don't turn the book in late.

Your New Job: Promoting Your Book

A cartoon by Roz Chast in the *New Yorker* shows a writer on the phone: "Mud-wrestle in my underwear on national TV while holding up a copy of my new book?" and he responds, "NO PROBLEMO!"

Maybe mud-wrestling is far-fetched, but nowadays the publisher might want you to, say, promise to tweet and update your Facebook page every fifteen minutes (I wish I were making that up). There is so much noise out there that publishers need your help to break through it—and your ability to reach potential readers can determine whether you get published at all. This is so important that an agent advised one of my students to start a blog and attract readers before writing a book.

Unless you are nationally famous (in which case your fame does it for you), these days you are expected to do more and more of the promotion for your book, from hiring publicists to setting up and paying for tours. Authors have turned out to be ingenious at this. Laurie Wagner, author of *Living Happily Ever After*, said that an aunt threw huge book parties for her in Los Angeles. "At the first event, I sold

160 books to family and friends. The next event I sold 120. And the events generate word of mouth."

When San Francisco's Kirk Read got his coming-of-age memoir, *How I Learned to Snap*, published by Hill Street Press, an independent house in Athens, Georgia, he understood that publishing it was all they could afford to do. "I told them, just send me two hundred books and I'll sell them," Read told me. He drove to one hundred tour dates in forty cities, everything from book group meetings to huge university lectures. He made purple T-shirts and buttons depicting a hand snapping and gave them out at each stop. He promoted his hardback so vigorously that Penguin bought the paperback rights.

Do-it-yourself promotion pays off, if not in huge sales then at least in keeping a good book in print long enough to find its readers. This is important in a day when bookstores give a book about three weeks on the shelf before they return it to the publisher. Linda Watanabe McFerrin of San Francisco, author of the story collection *The Hand of Buddha*, traveled to twenty-five states on an Amtrak pass for a month to promote it. She taught workshops and stayed with friends. Constance Hale, author of *Sin and Syntax: How to Craft Wickedly Effective Prose*, conducts writing and grammar workshops. "Each time I teach a class there's a little notice in some catalog or mailer about my book," she told me.

My friend Mark Childress, author of *One Mississippi*, told me that early in his career he drove across the country and tried to go in and shake hands with every bookstore owner in his path. Charles Frazier wrote to bookstores across the South saying they might be interested in his novel *Cold Mountain*. A friend of mine speaks at Rotary clubs, always making sure they have his books there for sale afterward. He even spoke to the American Glaucoma Society. "There are conventions and conferences in town all the time, and they need some alternative to their subjects," he told me.

One of the great overlooked book-selling circuits in the United States are the local chapters of Hadassah or Jewish women's groups. They're terrific at building word of mouth and sales. And you can make yourself available to book clubs, a gratifying transaction on both sides, because the book club is delighted to have a real live author to talk to, and the author is thrilled to speak to readers.

BLOGS CAN HELP YOU SELL A MEMOIR

Bloggers such as Mimi Smartypants, Pamela Ribon, Wendy McClure, and Jessica "Washingtonienne" Cutler have turned their blogs into book deals. Colby Buzzell, an American soldier, wrote a blog about his experiences as a machine-gunner in Iraq that became a book, *My War: Killing Time in Iraq*. Julie Powell wrote a cooking blog, the Julie/Julia Project, which became *Julie & Julia*, a bestselling book and then a movie with Meryl Streep. A Baghdad blogger named Salam Pax turned his online war diary from Iraq into a collection called *Salam Pax: The Clandestine Diary of an Ordinary Iraqi*. Ana Marie Cox, editor of Wonkette.com, sold her first novel, *Dog Days*, to Riverhead Books (with a $275,000 advance) on the strength of her blog audience.

Marrit Ingman had a hard time convincing publishers that her book on postpartum depression could sell. Then she asked readers of her blog to say why a book like that would interest them, and inserted their comments into the proposal. That convinced editors she already had an audience, and she sold her book, *Inconsolable*, to Seal Press.

Should You Self-Publish?

A staggering 764,448 titles were produced in 2009 by self-publishers and microniche publishers, according to R. R. Bowker. Many of them were produced online, at sites such as Lulu, Xlibris, and AuthorHouse. The number of traditionally published books? A more modest 288,355.

Confession time: One of those 764,448 titles was mine. There's a reason that the copyright page of this book says "revised edition." I self-published the first version. My other books were published in the traditional way. But when my first agent sent this one to New York, the editors said they loved it, but how, they said, were they supposed to sell a book in, say, Chicago, by someone no one in Chicago had ever heard of?

I got it. You have to get famous, then you can do a writing book. I had overlooked this little fact.

The heck with it, I decided. I had thousands of writing students in my files, and my name was still fairly well-known in the Bay Area, after my years as a columnist. Self-publishing has become in some ways a disarmingly easy proposition, or so it seemed to me. As long as you're doing the promoting, why not publish it yourself, too, and keep all the profits?

Certainly the first steps are simple. You upload a book onto one of the online book publishing sites, and a week later a book that looks a lot like any other published book arrives on your doorstep. It can cost about $8—less money than it costs to print out a manuscript at the local copy store.

It's so easy, and costs so little, that I like to surprise the authors whose manuscripts I've worked on by uploading their file and sending what looks like a published book. In fact that's a good way to cheer yourself up during the long slog of writing your book: Send yourself your manuscript in book form. Holding it in your hands will keep the dream alive—and also it's a great way to get a new perspective on what you've written.

Of course there's a lot more to it than simply uploading a file, if you want a book that doesn't scream homemade. The quality of the online presses isn't as good (you bend the cover and it stays bent) and they ship your books to you via FedEx, which costs the earth, instead of by freight, which is cheap.

Here's what I did: I hired editors to edit the text for me, and a professional designer to do the cover and the type. She emailed the book in a PDF file to a printer I'd found in Minneapolis. Three weeks later, the printer delivered one thousand books to me at a total printing and shipping cost of $2.61 a book. A man in a big truck double-parked outside my garage, and together he and I stacked the cartons against the wall. It was a very big stack. I couldn't even get to the paintbrushes or the gardening tools for a while. In fact it was while staring at all the boxes that I remembered I would have to somehow empty those boxes, book by book, into the hands of readers. And I couldn't even sell Kool-aid in the third grade. I'd say, "You don't want any Kool-Aid, do you?"

I did try. A friend had to walk me into Books Inc., on California Street here in San Francisco, but once I was there a man behind the counter got out a consignment order and took five books, and later called to ask for more. (Bookstores have these forms on hand for self-published authors these days.) I got some copies into other stores as well, but I couldn't make myself call them up later and ask if they needed any more books, and I could not make myself write invoices.

I did figure out how to put the book on Amazon. That's pretty easy, I must say, and the book seemed to sell pretty well there. The hardest part was having to periodically box up books and manhandle them down to the post office. Amazon is handy, though, because with a self-published book the main problem is distribution. You can't drive around to all the bookstores in the country. Even if the book gets some attention, the book won't be there when the reader goes to look for it. Getting that attention is difficult, too, because libraries won't buy self-published books, newspaper reviewers throw them in the mail bins on the floor, and bookstores are reluctant to schedule book signings.

So it's hard to personally duplicate what a publishing house does to edit, print, promote, and distribute a book. Yet it can make good sense to self-publish. Sometimes, as happened with this book, it will be picked up by a publisher after being available in self-published form for a while. Or take Lisa Genova, a Harvard PhD who wrote a novel about a woman with early-onset Alzheimer's disease. Turned down by the agents and editors she approached, she printed the book herself, and sold them out of the trunk of her car. Word spread; the book was picked up by a publisher, and *Still Alice* became a *New York Times* best seller.

If you can reach your market directly, without trying to figure out how to make the general population aware of your book, self-publishing can be just the ticket. I worked with David Gottfried, who decided to self-publish *Greed to Green*, his memoir of becoming a passionate green builder. He succeeded in getting the organization he founded, the U.S. Green Building Council, to underwrite the costs and sell it at conventions. Like many self-published authors, David found it difficult to get the book into bookstores, but through his own connections and website he had within four months sold the first printing of five thousand copies—a respectable result. He has since cleared $30,000 on the book and is about to bring out a second, *Greening My Life*.

It's also true that a self-published book that doesn't find a huge market can still be useful to its author. My student Lee Pryor said that his self-published *The Savvy Entrepreneur* got him an adjunct professor job at Tulane University and other perks that made it well worth it. He also put it on Amazon and sold hundreds of copies that way.

What If Mom Reads It?

As we're talking about activities that might lead to large numbers of strangers reading your book, we should talk about who's in it besides you, and what you've said about them. You can say anything you like about yourself, blab to the world that you drank morphine from a straw or did the Macarena on your father's grave. But what about the other people caught in your flashbulb? Will your sister be enchanted that you told the world she threw tampons over the neighbor's fence? Surely you won't be mentioning your mother's habit of stealing other people's Christmas decorations, will you?

It used to be that writers presented their experiences in the "thinly disguised autobiographical novel." Relatives depicted in them, however transparently, could say airily, "Like I would ever take a bath in champagne bought with the baby's milk money. What an imagination that girl has!" Now we call it a memoir (or personal essay). The writer steps out from behind the curtain and says it really happened. To me. Uh, to us. There's a lot of family underwear hanging out on the line. Before the book goes irrevocably into print, you will have to decide how much underwear you want up there, and whose.

If you worry about these other people objecting to your version of events, though, don't. Here's the thing to keep in mind: It's not what happened to you that's significant, but what you *think* happened to you. It's what you remember, and why you remember things that way. Any story of what happened is always a version of what happened. The Anita Hills have their version, the Clarence Thomases have theirs, and truth turns out to be a snowflake, no two alike. But memory is a rock. It is your version of what happened to you.

My twin sister, Adrian, read *Hold Me Close*, which had a subplot about our father. She wrote this about the book to our mother:

> While I was reading Adair's book, the one thing that
> struck me was how different events were in my mind than
> in Adair's. I started out saying to myself, "Hey, that
> didn't happen that way," but after a while I realized it
> wasn't my book. Adair made herself the hero in places
> about Dad in ways I didn't think were accurate. But it's
> her book—I guess she can make herself the hero. When I
> write a book, I can make myself the hero, too.

Now is the time to read through the manuscript with them in mind. To offer them privacy, you will probably be changing or disguising some identifying details. You can change the names of friends, and sometimes omit names of relatives ("My aunt told me"). Your husband's brother can appear as a man called Don, "an engineer in his forties." Or you can assign a story you heard from one person to someone else. If the gender doesn't matter, you can even change the sex (the therapist you thought was a loon could be changed to a man). In my memoir, only the names of my immediate family and of my siblings are real—the rest are changed. Morgan's boyfriend had a perfect name—it killed me to have to change it.

Do change the details rather than withhold them. I read a manuscript in which the author has declined to state not only any identifying details but even what *country* she grew up in. That approach will guarantee her no fallout from outraged relatives, chiefly because the resulting tale is too murky to be published.

It's hard to disguise close relatives, of course. You can't say, "My father, let's call him Ned." My own mother was great when *Hold Me*

Close came out. She didn't need to read my sister's note, above—she knew perfectly well she was in it. She worked in a bookstore, and offered to sign my book when people came in. But she didn't read it. She had by then logged more than a few hours as the mother of a writer. She didn't want to get mad at me.

But we all can't hope for the maturely detached reader, the flattered one (yes, there are plenty of those), or the absent one. If an anecdote will hurt somebody, and it's not crucial to your story, consider taking it out. Why say your brother spent time in prison if the story is about the six years you spent in Nepal? Your brother, like all of us, works hard at trying to have some say over the self he presents to the world, and he wants to keep it that way.

What to do? Wait until all your relatives are dead?

Consider Your Options

Before we take a look at some of your options, it's important to discuss the legalities of naming other people in your memoir. Not walloping people in print is a matter of conscience and decency, but it does also have its legal aspects. Augusten Burroughs's family sued him for certain details in *Running with Scissors*, including saying that his father burned his forehead with a cigarette when Burroughs was six.

For a portrait to be "actional," as they call it—meaning it is libel—it must be so accurate that a reader would have no problem linking the incompetent doctor in the story with the one who actually treated the narrator for breast cancer. Like my publisher, yours might ask your family to sign releases. My ex-husband, husband, and both kids had to sign one. (They didn't ask my mother to, thank goodness. She'd say, "I don't think so, Adair," and I'd end up having to take out the pivotal scene where my mother convinces Morgan that the whole family will be mad at her if she doesn't shape up.)

If you have concerns about any of the people you named (or even renamed) in your book, you may want to seek legal counsel from an attorney who specializes in publication law. At the very least, you should discuss the issue with your agent and editor.

Okay, let's say your agent and editor are on board, but you still need to deal with those potentially restless relatives or other people mentioned in your book. Below are a few possible options: let's take a quick look at each of them.

INCLUDE AN AUTHOR'S NOTE

Suggest in an author's note that you are relying on memory or that some relatives would disagree with your account of things. This will allow your father to say you made the whole thing up, although of course you didn't. One author writes, "Out of concern for the privacy of others, names have been changed and identities disguised. To enliven the narrative, I merge a few events in time, leap and fill in gaps in memories about sequence and details, and reconstruct dialogue that I could not possibly remember verbatim."

ASK PERMISSION

Novelist Annie Dillard has said she lets her relatives read her books and take out anything they don't like. (Dillard's last novel was a description of the landscape.) Dave Eggers sent the manuscript of *A Heartbreaking Work of Staggering Genius* to people mentioned in it and let them make revisions. "You have to choose who you're okay with pissing off," he said. He even put phone numbers in the first edition, though he took them out in later editions.

Sometimes asking the permission of someone who loves you is emotional blackmail, though. You ask permission, but can they say no? "Here, I wrote this whole book, is it okay to publish or should I throw it away?" I was certainly uncomfortably aware of that when showing the manuscript of *Hold Me Close* to Morgan.

In an essay called "Other People's Secrets," memoirist Patricia Hampl recalls how she always thought that a poem she wrote outing her mother as an epileptic helped rid her mother of a guilty secret. Then Hampl learned that her mother always hated that poem, and allowed it to be published anyway only because she wanted to help her daughter succeed as a writer. "I am trying now to remember if I cared about her feelings at all," Hampl said in an essay written years later. She had argued with her mother into letting her use the poem by saying, "I will cut it if you really want me to," *beat*, "but it's the best poem in the book."

BRIBE THEM

You're getting paid—spread the loot around. David Sedaris wrote in *Naked* about his mother's death from cancer and his sister's first period. He told the *New York Times*, "The publisher made everyone sign a waiver saying they wouldn't sue me. At Christmastime, I took a big stack of gifts and said, 'Everybody, these are your presents and this is the release form—just sign here.'"

Morgan got 10 percent of my royalties for the memoir I wrote about her. (My son, Patrick, claimed he should get some money, too. "If I hadn't been so good," he argued, "your book would have been a pile of psychotic scribblings.")

CHANGE YOUR NAME

Publishers hate pen names. They may want you to go on tour and promote the book, which is difficult when you are keeping your true identity a secret. And how flattering are veils, really?

As a last resort, you can legally change your own name. Lisa Michaels, whose dad was a weatherman whom she had reason to believe the FBI were still interested in, changed all the names in *Split*, her book about being a child of radical 1960s parents. Including her own! She legally changed her name to Michaels—and then her husband took her new name. They're the Michaels family.

DON'T WRITE IT

Martha Sherrill had a contract to write a memoir about her father, a well-known polling expert, when in the midst of her research, "A massive skeleton popped right out of the closet," as she told the *New York Times*. She turned her back on a lucrative, attention-getting memoir and instead wrote a novel called *The Ruins of California*. "I suppose I could have done that book," she said. "It would have been shocking and I could have gotten all kinds of attention . . . but I'm really attached to my family."

So much trouble, writing a book, getting it published, worrying about who's in it! Why on earth do we writers put ourselves through all this? For the answer to that, turn to the epilogue.

POSTSCRIPT

What You Get When You Write from Life

Whether you can really draw or not, whether you can really act or not, or write or not, just trying to do it always gives you a different relationship to meaning.

—ANNA DEAVERE SMITH IN *LETTERS TO A YOUNG ARTIST*

WE'VE TALKED a lot about how to write essays and memoirs. But we haven't talked about *why* we do this—why writing seems so valuable, so worthwhile, so exciting, why it is worth all the classes, all the discouragement, all the drafts and then all the effort of getting the work out there where it can be read. We could be knitting, gardening, piling up money in the bank, going sailing with everybody else, instead of hunching over a table, typing letters onto a screen.

Obviously the thrill of being published is part of it, not to mention the possibility of fame and a villa in France and impressing everyone you know. But writing a memoir or an essay or anything else that allows you to reflect on your life, has benefits that go far beyond being published. It does all kinds of things for the inside of your head, and for your heart. It sets you free in the world, wherever your body might be forced to pitch its tent. In *Tiger's Eye*, a memoir about her illness, Inga Clendinnen said, "Being able to make a story from nothing instead of concocting it out of elusive memories made me happy. It also relieved my fear of being trapped 'inside.' My labeled body might be lying on my labeled bed, but my mind could be anywhere, keeping whatever company I chose."

WRITING ENRICHES YOU

Susan Parker, author of *Tumbling After*, had never written anything until her husband Ralph broke his neck in a bicycle accident while pedaling down Grizzly Peak near Berkeley, California. Ralph Hager was a retired nuclear physicist; she was in her early forties, thirteen years younger. The accident left Ralph a quadriplegic and Susan a caregiver, with instructions to catheterize her husband every four hours twenty-four hours a day. "My life was wrecked after Ralph's accident. There was nothing left of it. Writing gave me a new sense of self worth, new friends. Ralph is proud of me. I'm in an MFA program. My life is so much richer than it was before."

WRITING GIVES YOU BACK YOUR PAST

Memoir is, after all, French for *memory*. You get back, in vivid new form on the page, your own memories: how your housepainter dad would come home, blow his nose, and show your mother the colors that accumulated from painting all day. Or how your relatives lived with you when you were all poor, and one day you got stuck on a newly glued toilet while your uncles and aunts beat on the door.

One of my students, Kathy Briccetti-Clark of Oakland, said, "I am writing things I have wanted to get down ever since they happened to me twenty and thirty years ago. I'm trying to capture the dim lighting and the smells of mildew, gym shoes, and perfume in my high school locker."

Writing also reshapes your past. Aren't the stories you've written down funnier, sharper now than when they actually happened? And haven't the vivid new versions taken the place in your head of those old, chaotic, depressing memories? Writing lets you take your memories and transform them; they may have entered your mind in a free fall, landing there and becoming a part of you, but they leave in a controlled descent.

WRITING CHANGES YOUR RELATIONSHIPS

To write well, you have to think about your relatives as characters, with secret thoughts and passions of their own—not as villains (twirling mustaches and train tracks). You gain perspective into them, and thus into their role in shaping your life. My friend Tina Martin said to me, "Do you have to respond as a victim to a father who really didn't do his job? I think it's wonderful when someone can get something not offered from a relationship. Don't we all create our own stories and imagine our own relationships?"

WRITING GIVES BOUNDARY TO THE PAIN

The perspective writing gives you on your own life is convenient. Once when I picked up Morgan the Bad (my teenaged daughter) at the police station, I noticed how the vending machine in the lobby kept flashing "Have a Nice Day" in red digital letters while they were fetching her for me. I was crying, but I was also, in the back of my mind, taking note of that ironic detail, the flashing vending machine. Being a writer helped that night. It helps on many days and nights. (And it's much, much cheaper than therapy.)

You begin to get distance from an event the moment you write it down. At some point, even the most intimate and horrendous details of your life become transformed into material. When you pin your misfortune to the page, you rob it of its power. Isabel Allende, who wrote a memoir about the death of her daughter called *Paula: A Memoir*, told me, "Writing is always a joyful process. You go into a quiet place inside you, and you transform something that may be very painful into words. It gives boundary to the pain. It sorts out the confusion. It helps you to understand, and, finally, to accept."

Writing can literally save your life. Tim O'Brien, author of *The Things They Carried*, was contemplating suicide one night, and as he thought about it, he wrote about it. "I'd literally leave the typewriter and go to the balcony, and think about jumping off, and go back and type another sentence."

A woman in my class, haunted for eight years by the unsolved murder of her husband, wrote herself a new story in which she is not the aging, lonely widow, but a vibrant woman with a lot to offer the world.

WRITING GIVES YOU JOY

When you set your stories down, that very act charges up every part of you, makes you feel alive, important, satisfied. You feel enlarged, fed, painted in brighter colors by what you have chosen to say about yourself, by the sheer fun of watching amazing words come out of your fingertips, words that were never in the world before. Recently, one of my writing students emailed me to say:

```
There are those days when I know I've gained thirty-
five pounds overnight. There will be no hike, not even
a walk, no leaving the house, no getting dressed and
probably not even any getting out of bed. And then, I
think, I can write in bed. I don't even have to wash my
face, not even brush my teeth. I can scratch away at
some exercise with abandon, and I have to say, sometimes
I can't get over how funny and cute I think I am. After
an hour or so, I often feel I've lost enough weight to
get dressed! And maybe, maybe even leave the house.
```

WRITING LETS YOU FIND OUT WHAT YOU THINK

Part of the pleasure of writing is finding out what you think. In the process of trying to say clearly what you mean, about growing up as an American child with a Korean face, or having to finally let go of your marriage, or render the experience of being a drug therapist in a county jail, you learn; and as you learn you shape your character, for who are you, if not what you have learned? As E. B. White said, "The practice and habit of writing not only drain the mind but supply it, too."

WRITING CHANGES WHAT YOU SEE

As a writer, you notice everything: the dog who right now is noisily dismantling a paper cup under the table, the mysterious white goo on your husband's hair, how your ex-husband cried until his nose bled all over his blue shirt and blue sweater and you had to mop him up with tissues and say, "No more poetry at the dinner table."

You become like a photographer who takes his camera with him everywhere, looking for color and contrast and interesting juxtapositions. Because you have that camera, you see not just the houses but the light on them. That's not a bad thing, noticing the light.

WRITING GIVES YOUR LIFE MEANING

Real life, after all, is just one thing after another: sprinklers left on, a pain down the arm, a death, getting stuck in jobs and relationships, spots of joy, vague defeats, unexpected events. You don't marry the love of your life, or if you do, it doesn't work out. You work hard, but never make CEO anyway. You move to ten different cities and it's the same damn thing.

But when viewed through binoculars from the hilltop—that is, with the perspective that writing can bestow—those same events gain order and coherence. The result is not life faithfully recorded but life made sense of, redeemed, enriched. Every decision you make when shaping your story (what to include, what to leave out, what to mute, what to emphasize) begins the process of transforming random events into a story with meaning and resolution, thus transforming your life in the same way. "Life is a hopelessly meager thing," my father said. "What counts is what we dream into it, the words we find to describe it when we arrange jarring details to make a pleasing whole."

A friend of mine was suffering from depression. He had lost several close friends to AIDS and carried around memories of a brutal childhood in foster care. He took a creative writing class in which the teacher invited each student to write the story of his life as an epic fairy tale with himself as the hero. Doing that assignment transformed Michael's life. He had always seen himself as the victim of his own story. Now he saw himself as the hero. He saw, too, that as the hero he had the power to change the ending. He set about doing just that.

WRITING LETS YOU SHARE

Once the writing has helped you figure things out, you share your insights with others who might need it. William Styron discovered this when he wrote an article about the pain of severe depression that turned into the memoir *Darkness Visible*. "The overwhelming reactions made me feel that I had helped unlock a closet from which many souls were eager to come out and proclaim that they, too, had experienced the feelings I had described." Styron concluded that to educate his audience about depression represented a worthwhile reason to have invaded his own privacy.

Kirk Read, author of *How I Learned to Snap*, told me it's not easy to go home again when your home is Lexington, Kentucky, and you've written a candid gay memoir. "But it all boils down to gay fourteen-year-olds in small towns," he went on. "If they can get their hands on the book, and it helps them even a little bit, then my being uncomfortable at my church's Christmas Eve service is a tiny matter."

After *Hold Me Close* came out, I got mail from mothers going through what I had, and those letters mattered to me. A woman named Louise Seeley said, "You've reminded me that the only thing I can do is the best I can, love my son, and never give up."(Admittedly, another reader called *Hold Me Close* "a powerful birth control device.")

Write it down. Whatever it is, write it down. Chip it into marble. Type it into Microsoft Word. Spell it out in seaweeds on the shore. We are each of us an endangered species, delicate as unicorns.

APPENDIX

Here are some additional resources for you, from books that I think will help aspiring writers furnish their heads to writing suggestions to computer tips.

Reading List

Here's a short and subjective list of memoirs you might enjoy.

And When Did You Last See Your Father? by Blake Morrison
Angela's Ashes by Frank McCourt
Borstal Boy by Brendan Behan
The Color of Water: A Black Man's Tribute to His White Mother by James McBride
Growing Up by Russell Baker
The Liars' Club by Mary Karr
Lit by Mary Karr
Memoirs of a Catholic Girlhood by Mary McCarthy
The Only Girl in the Car by Kathy Dobie
This Boy's Life by Tobias Wolff

Useful Texts

It's amazing how many books on writing there are out there. Some are useful, some less so. (I have spared you the titles that urge you to "move around the room in a joyful way.") Below are a few, though, that I recommend.

The Art of the Personal Essay by Philip Lopate
Bird by Bird by Anne Lamott (the very best of the inspirational writing books)

The Making of a Story by Alice LaPlante (a comprehensive book with excellent exercises and examples)

The Situation and the Story by Vivian Gornick (this book by a veteran memoirist shows that you use the particular circumstances of your tale—the situation—to tell a universal human story)

Unreliable Truth: On Memoir and Memory by Maureen Murdock

Writing Fiction: A Guide to Narrative Craft (any edition) by Janet Burroway (Find it secondhand or it'll cost the earth. Aimed at fiction writers, but of course the principles are the same. I discovered my sister reading this at a campsite and was forced to confiscate it as I needed it more than she did.)

Your Life as Story by Tristine Rainer

Writing Exercises

Most of the prompts below are ones that I've assigned often enough to know they almost always lead to interesting, and highly specific, sketches or whole essays. ("Write about the contents of your closet," for example, has resulted in at least fifteen published essays.)

GENERAL

Write a piece that takes place in a single time period: washing a car, packing a suitcase, cleaning a refrigerator, choosing an outfit for an important event.

Write about your mother's jewelry (or lack thereof).

Where—or who—is home for you?

Write about an early memory. What did you feel at the time of the event? Go through the senses of touch, smell, sight, hearing, and taste. Invent the details you don't remember. Why do you suppose you still remember this moment after all these years, when you have forgotten so much else?

Write about your father's car.

Describe a journey you took. Tell where you broke down, where you slept, ate, and visited. Make the story evocative of your mood at the time, and show us what changed.

Begin a piece with the sentence, "I fell in love with my life one Tuesday in August." You can change the day and the month, of course, unless you did have a transporting experience on a Tuesday in August.

Tell a personal story that takes place within a larger public story: September 11, a blackout, Obama's inauguration, an earthquake. Invent the details that you don't remember: "It was a Friday, so I was probably on my way to school . . ."

Write about a new passion that's unlike you: growing roses or following the stock market or shooting a gun.

You dropped dead suddenly and your house is cleared out. What do they find?

You saw your mother differently, even if only for a moment.

What skill did you never learn? My ex-husband never learned to ride a bicycle, for example. I never learned to put on eyeliner.

Write about the time your name wasn't on the list.

Write a piece about cleaning something out: a fridge, a drawer, a room, a garage. Let us see in the piece that you're not just physically making space, but that you're also making mental space, letting go of an old self and making room for a new one.

If you have lost a parent, write on this subject:

> I forgot to tell my mother . . .
> I forgot to tell my father . . .

Write a list of ten to twenty ways in which you do something odd: in dress, in eating, in driving, in thinking, in hobbies, superstitious behavior, anything. "I never give up on a piece of clothing," or "I would rather try to carry ten plastic grocery bags in each hand than take two trips to bring my groceries in."

Use a succession of objects to tell your life story: cars you have owned, houses you've lived in, your T-shirts, coffee cups, couches. Or list the songs that were playing at the different phases of your life.

Tell your life story in quotes, as in these examples:

> "You have to put your face underwater so you can swim," she said, and shoved my head into the enamel dishpan.

> "Go ahead, say I blasted your life at a tender age. There must be some way we can get famous," my father said as he handed me back the pages of my memoir.

Write a page about what you are most afraid of. Use images—no generalizations!

Describe a procedure from start to finish—something you do at work or at home. Be precise, but don't be afraid to mix in other elements—tone, flashbacks, revealing anecdotes. (I am thinking of writing something inspired by my two grown kids called "The Art of Unpacking a Box.")

Identify ten moments in your life after which something in you changed irrevocably. Write a half page on each. Use these as springboards for essays.

List specific images and details about an event, then pick the best ones and add new ones as they occur. Don't state the meaning, but allow the details to reveal it.

Write about the contents of your closet. Who did you buy that rabbit fur coat for? And those tall spiked black boots, the ones that were going to change your life? How many of the clothes fit you, or fit who you are now? Be specific.

Write one short anecdote from each year of your life, starting with the earliest memory you have.

Write a list of ten things you will certainly never write about. Write a paragraph on each. You can begin, "I will never talk about the day when [insert experience] and even if I do, I will never tell anybody the truth about that, which is [insert truth]."

Jot down the events of your life under categories: events, people, secret thoughts, familiar objects. Which of those still haunt you? Write about them.

Write about an object. Maybe one that has gone from house to house with you, or one that has stood still while your life changed (kitchen table?). Stick close to the object, and see if a story emerges.

Write an instruction manual called "How to Be Me."

MEMOIR EXERCISES

Get out your family albums. Pick out a number of photographs, one or two from each period of your life, arrange them in a stack like a deck of cards, with the earliest photo on top and the latest on the bottom. Pick up the first and start writing. Tell your reader what's in the photograph, what it doesn't show, what happened just before or just after it was taken.

Write a short but complete piece (1,000 words maximum) that spans a large amount of time (at least ten years) in your life. Avoid generalization and abstraction.

Write a list of details from your childhood. My own list would include milk delivered in glass bottles, metal ice cube trays with levers, cap guns, hula hoops, linoleum flooring patterned to look like bricks, and play guns made out of clothespins.

out an old family photo and write about what's in the frame and about what's not in the frame. What happened before or after the picture was taken? What does the writer know now that the people in the photograph didn't know then?

In the Stanislavski acting method, every character in a drama has a central desire or objective—a motivation—that drives him through each scene and through the story. What desire drives each of the main characters in your memoir?

Not sure what your desire line is? Try writing a synopsis, narrating the events of your story in prose. "This is a story about a woman who falls passionately in love with a man and then sacrifices her talents and her professional ambitions to help him become successful. In doing so, they grow apart and she becomes irrelevant to him. She becomes bitter and resentful while he becomes absorbed in his own career. The more successful he becomes the less he needs her and the more needy she becomes."

Draw the floor plan of a house you lived in. Or of your childhood neighborhood, the streets, houses, and so on, putting in notes about incidents as you remember them.

Write two pages of backstory about your parents. What happens before the events your book portrays?

Write a scene in which one character wants something that the other does not want to give.

IDEAS FOR HOLIDAY ESSAYS

Write about your worst Valentine's Day.

Write about your family's method of decorating the Christmas tree.

Write about something that happened to you on Halloween. Or at a Halloween party or while shopping for a costume at Goodwill. Or give us the day when your cheapskate mother pinned maple leaves all over you, told you to tell people you were Autumn, and sent you rustling off to the first grade.

Write about what you're doing for Thanksgiving and what will almost certainly go wrong. Who won't be there, who will be there, and why? Who is doing the cooking?

Write a holiday newsletter in which you list the ways in which you and others in your family have, once again this year, failed to achieve anything worth mentioning in a holiday newsletter. Let us know your Uncle Albert was finally carted off to an institution and that your brother scandalized everybody by wearing brogans with a skirt to the opera (when everyone knows that's too heavy a shoe to wear with a skirt). Make fun of yourself. If you actually had some accomplishments this year, keep it to yourself, please—nobody wants to hear it.

Write ten cranky specific tips for someone buying Christmas or Hanukkah presents for you.

HUMOR EXERCISES

Take any commonly accepted idea and reverse it. Write about the benefits of being mugged, fired, sick, divorced, broke, stood up.

Write a letter of complaint. My friend Joan Frank did this when she wrote an essay in the form of a letter to a panty hose manufacturer. It starts out as a conventional letter of complaint: "So this is to return the enclosed $3.69-plus-tax product, your sheer-to-waist, Sublime Soiree, Midnight Smoke pantyhose . . ." She explains at length that she did not buy the wrong size or throw the nylons in the washing machine and by the time the essay is done the nylons manufacturer has been treated to a pretty thorough review of the frantic, money-strapped modern woman's lot in life, a lot she was able to bear until this final thing happened, and she got a run in her new stockings.

Tell us, in one page, why you are so delightful to live with (irony here, please).

Write three apologies. Example:

To Gabrielle:

I'm sorry that I stepped on your hamster. I was too embarrassed to tell you how he died that night. I was only seven. It was like stepping on a warm beanbag, a small crunch of softness.

DETAIL AND IMAGE EXERCISES

Write a list of fifty images for a piece you're working on or thinking about.

Write down thirty images from a typical day. Include anything that strikes you: overheard snatches of conversation, graffiti, the sights and smells and textures of your day.

Write a piece that begins with a foreboding smell.

Describe a setting that has changed over time—one family home sold to remodelers, a forest or farm turned housing development, a city block demolished for a freeway. Focus on the details of the place, including weather, geography, people, and machines, letting those details imply your feelings about the change. Or describe a setting that has remained the same, but let readers see how your description of it reflects changes that have occurred in you over time.

Choose three from the following list, and write one hundred words on each, telling us what memories the smell evokes for you. Use all five senses: smell, taste, hearing, sight, and touch.

Melted tar   Tobacco
Noxzema   Exhaust
Suntan lotion   Lunch box
Bug spray   Play-Doh

Take three pages of one of your pieces and put an image in every single sentence.

Describe an object that you associate with a particular family member: a pipe, a bathrobe, a baseball glove.

Go somewhere you have never been—a biker bar, a library, a hardware store, a baby shower, a church, a lesson, a meeting—and write what you find out about yourself by being in that strange or boring or intimidating environment. It could be just going out to dinner by yourself if you have never done that before.

REVISION EXERCISES

Start with something very small. A friend of mine was assigned to rewrite an article on unlawful detainer and discovered a way to do it: "I stuck a piece of paper in my typewriter and started correcting the minor mistakes. The correction of one minor mistake led to correcting another, and the authority I had to cite to correct that mistake led to finding another mistake. I ended up rewriting that whole article."

Write a one-page description of something you're working on, and talk about what is perplexing you most.

Take a draft of a piece of yours, edit it to half its length, then write it back to its original length, putting in new stuff to fill the holes you made. In the first draft you write what people expect you to write— what you expect yourself to write. It's the second, third, fourth draft that really makes you dig deeper. That's when you say something we don't expect you to say, that even you didn't expect you to say.

Print out a piece and cut it apart with a pair of scissors, just as an experiment, shoving paragraphs around to see if a different order would be interesting. (You might find that your first paragraph is actually your last, or vice versa.)

Print your piece out with line breaks so that each paragraph is now on a page by itself, and thus stands out clearly, with all its glories and flaws. Edit.

KITCHEN-TIMER EXERCISES

For fifteen minutes, start every sentence with "I remember" or "I don't remember" or "I wish."

Freewrite for ten minutes, allowing whatever images and subjects that come up onto the page. Begin with this phrase: "Everything was fine until..."

When you finish, go over your freewriting and highlight four key words or images. Now do four more ten-minute exercises using the highlighted words and images as springboards. Again, let the writing go where it will. When you finish, read over all drafts. Cut and paste the best sentences together into a single piece.

INSPIRATIONAL EXERCISES

Choose a favorite essay (that you did not write) and type it into your computer word for word. You'll see how the author did it.

Get a big empty box and throw your story ideas in there one by one as you jot them down.

In *13 Ways of Looking at the Novel*, Jane Smiley tells the story of a woman named Ilene Beckerman, who published *Love, Loss, and What I Wore*. "Her initial impulse had been to jot down some memories from the early days of her marriage for her children, herself, and her best friend," said Smiley, "so she kept paper and pencils at hand, and every time she remembered something, she wrote it out. Sometimes it was a few pages long, other times only a page. She did not write about the memories in any particular order, only when they occurred to her. She filed each page with the others in a manila folder, and after a year she pulled out the folder, read over the pages, organized them chronologically, and had them typed. She made five copies—one for herself and each of her three children, and one for her best friend. Some months after she was finished, the phone rang. It was her best friend, who asked her whether she would mind talking to a publisher about publishing her memoir."

Smiley points out that "one thing to understand about this anecdote is that she wasn't merely lucky, it was also that she believed in what she was writing—she found it valuable, interesting, and worthwhile, if only as a private record, and she considered herself capable of achieving her goal."

Tricks of the (Computer) Trade

Here are a few of my favorite tips and techniques to try out on the computer. If you already know about them, great. If not, your life is about to get much, much easier.

SEARCH

Want to find something you wrote that has disappeared into the bowels of your computer? To find where you wrote about, say, your canary, Lola, go to the Start menu on the computer task bar and click on the little icon of a magnifying glass followed by the word *Search*. (Mac users should click on the magnifying glass icon in the upper right corner of their screen; a search box called Spotlight will pop up.) You can search for not only for the name of any file ("Lola") by typing in a keyword, but also any word in any file (*canary*). Just try to remember a unique phrase in that file.

PASTE SPECIAL

For years, I couldn't figure out how to get rid of all the crazy fonts that popped up in a document, thanks to my bad habit of cutting and pasting sections from old files. I knew how to use the Paste tool, but that merely cloaks the old formatting—it's still there and will reappear when you move stuff. Would I have to type stuff all over again, just to permanently change the formatting? In this high-tech day and age? No! I highlight the section with the crazy font, cut it, and then paste it back in using Paste Special (under Edit in Microsoft Word), choosing Unformatted. Whoo-ee! I can also highlight the section and click on Edit, then Clear, then Formats. This technique also gets rid of any indelible highlighting.

THE OFFICE CLIPBOARD

The clipboard tool is under Edit in Microsoft Word. (For Mac users, it's called Scrapbook and you'll find it in the Tools menu.) Open it and you can cut or copy up to twenty-four items of any length in a holding tank beside your document. This means that when you cut a paragraph to move it, you can park it in the clipboard temporarily. Very, very handy.

PROTECT YOUR WORK

Maxine Hong Kingston lost an entire book in the Berkeley fire. The easiest way to prevent that is to regularly email your files to yourself— they'll be safe in cyberspace even if your whole state burns down. There are also services you can sign up for that lift all new files from your computer every night and store them safely on servers elsewhere.

CONTRIBUTORS

SPECIAL THANKS to the friends, colleagues, and writing students I have quoted in this book:

Christina Boufis, Katherine Brennan, Janis Cooke Newman, Barbara Cressman, Melody Cryns, Linda Curtis, Kathleen Denny, Nancy Devine, Robert Doane, Joan Frank, Lynn Freed, Rita Hargrave, Carol Lena Figueiredo, Wendy Lichtman, Kristin Lund, Hank Martinson, Susan Parker, Lucas Peltonen, Lisa Pongrace, Metece Riccio, Holly Rose, Scottie Ross, Stan Sinberg, Ellie Spence, Evelyn Strauss, Chris Voisard, Bonnie Wach, Cecilia Worth

INDEX

ABOUT THE AUTHOR

ADAIR LARA started her career by writing for local magazines—first as managing editor of *San Francisco Focus*, the city magazine, and then as executive editor of *SF*, a design magazine at which she passed herself off as someone passionately interested in interior design. She wrote a column every Tuesday and Thursday for the *San Francisco Chronicle* for twelve years, winning the Associated Press Award for Best Columnist in California, and was a reporter in the paper's books and features department for four years more.

She has published more than ten books and is a contributor to magazines such as *MORE*, *Reader's Digest*, *Glamour*, and *Ladies' Home Journal*. Lara leads sold-out writing workshops and does private memoir consulting in the San Francisco Bay Area. She lives in San Francisco with her husband, Bill LeBlond. For more, visit www.adairlara.com.

Photo by Johanna Jhanda